Solving Organizational Problems

*A Proven Method for Groups to
Permanently Resolve Difficult,
Complex, and Persistent Problems*

SECOND EDITION

CHRIS CHRISTENSEN

Ordering Information:

For orders and inquiries, please contact:
1-888-375-9818
www.toplinkpublishing.com
bookorder@toplinkpublishing.com

Printed in the United States of America

Contents

1. Introduction

Why another book on problem solving? There have been hundreds of books on this topic printed already. In fact, most adults already know how to solve problems—it is impossible to reach maturity without solving many problems. So what good can another book on this subject provide?

First, based upon my observations as a business consultant, I believe some of the methods for solving problems used in my client's organizations are not as effective as they could be. The process shown in this book addresses the major shortcomings that I have seen in those organizations that fail to resolve persistent, organizational problems.

Second, while everyone in an organization knows how to solve problems, they solve them in many different ways. When a technical or an executive team sets out to solve a problem, however, it needs to follow a *single* approach. Otherwise, the problem solvers waste time and undermine the collaboration necessary to resolve problems efficiently. In this book, I describe a single process from beginning to end. The process includes various tools such as creativity exercises or team voting methods that may be utilized at various parts of the process. In my opinion, this method represents the best approach that groups can use to permanently solve those problems that seem to never go away no matter how many times and how much money is spent trying to solve them.

The problem-solving process I propose differs from others in many ways. Here are four salient distinctions:

1. *Attention to identifying key problems.* In this seven-step process, more time is spent determining which problem to solve before expending money, time, and effort to solve it. Accordingly, people

trying to solve a problem have a better understanding of the importance of the problem they are solving and the feasibility of potential solutions, so they are better equipped to prioritize their work.

2. *Defining problems in ways that expand choices for solutions.* Problems are defined in a fashion that actually increases opportunities for solutions rather than reducing the number of them.

3. *Attention to multiple causes of problems.* This seven-step process does not seek and does not settle for identifying a single root cause of any problem— rather, the complete set of root causes is surfaced and eliminated.

4. *Emphasis on implementation of solutions.* Unlike nearly all of the other approaches documented in books and trade journals, this process includes a practical step that forces the problem-solving team to persuade management to incorporate those changes necessary to permanently solve the problem. The problem is not considered solved until the necessary changes are enacted to ensure that the problem is—and stays—solved.

My hope is that managers will adopt this problem-solving process to resolve the most pressing and troublesome issues that the organization confronts. In addition to recommending a single, effective problem-solving process (chapter three), I discuss how an organization can change its culture so that problems can surface more efficiently and become permanently resolved (chapter four). Also provided are case studies to show some results that teams have achieved by using the process (chapter five).

The process for solving problems described in this book developed over many years. As a manager in industry for three decades and then as a business consultant for two more decades, I have led or guided many groups through problem-solving activities. I learned to apply steps from many disciplines to actual situations in real organizations. Some of the techniques I tried from Total Quality Management, Six Sigma, Lean Operations, Operational Excellence, Design for Excellence, Business Process Improvement, and other management initiatives worked better than others. Accordingly, I experimented with improvements to the problem-solving process over time until it became what I share in this book.

I have confidence that the problem-solving approach I describe is both effective and practical. I have watched it actually cause changes in many organizations that improved profits, increased customer satisfaction, lowered operating costs, improved employee satisfaction, and alleviated management stress.

Primarily, for the past two decades I have observed these improvements to business operations as the result of workshops that I have conducted on-site at many organizations. The workshops typically take two days with a week or two in between them. I introduce the process to a problem-solving team that either selects a problem to address or is given one by its management. Together we develop a set of solutions, including recommendations for changes that need to be made in the organization in order to fully resolve the problem.

During the last two hours of the last session, the problem-solving team presents their recommendations to the decision-makers and receives immediate feedback. A few times the recommendations were adopted during the workshop, but more often, the managers asked for more research and offered some considerations of which the problem-solving team was not aware during the workshop. In nearly all cases, the senior managers have ultimately adopted a revised version of the recommendations made by the problem-solving team and the organization has benefited. I have never experienced a situation in which management has rejected the recommendations out of hand.

Problem Solving in an Agile Organization

Many organizations today have adopted a strategy of agile in difference to the structured approach upon which older businesses were built. The agile approach is not merely a slight variation of the structured approach, a "spin on an old theme." To the contrary, agile represents a significant change in the culture of the organization. Instead of systematically developing a plan and then executing that plan as rigorously as possible, agile businesses "try things out" and continuously modify products, services, and processes. For example, rather than develop a detailed design for a new product, the agile business creates a strawman or prototype and by repeatedly tinkering and adjusting it, improves its design until it satisfies its intended customer.

There is no doubt that the agile approach to business is appropriate. Many organizations have significantly enhanced their customers' satisfaction, shortened development times, and improved their profits by embracing agile.

In fact, the agile approach is the most intuitive one human beings try in solving problems. When faced with a problem, we nearly always try to imagine a solution and try out that solution or at least mentally explore how effective we believe the solution might be. If a rapidly identified, intuitive possible solution works, we should not apply a more structured problem solving methodology. My intention is never to complicate the problem solving practice. As the subtitle of this book implies, the method described in this book is intended to solve problems which cannot be solved simply and quickly. The method described here is intended for difficult, complex, and persistent problems.

Problem Solving and Critical Thinking

In addition to agile, another contemporary trend in business is critical thinking. Many corporations and agencies are devoting time and resources to encouraging, training, and nurturing a culture of critical thinking. Here are the seven characteristics that many modern organizations are attempting to instill in their workforces:

1. Challenging and questioning ideas
2. Surfacing assumptions underlying the organization's practices
3. Demanding evidence to support assertions
4. Understanding how statistics have been employed to treat all data presented
5. Recognizing biases
6. Predicting consequences and forecasting results of proposed actions and decisions
7. Understanding how humans think, process information, and make decisions

Problem solving is integral to critical thinking. In instances when an intuitive solution isn't effective, when problems turn out to be difficult, complex, and persistent, it is essential that a thoughtful and structured approach to solving those problems should be applied. The method described in this book incorporates the elements identified above and will help to create and reinforce a critical thinking culture.

2. Why Problem-Solving Processes Often Fail

Why do organizations fail to solve their problems? I have isolated ten key reasons that cause organizations to be unable to remove problems and keep them resolved. I also indicate how to prevent each of these roadblocks.

1. *Everyone knows how to solve problems, but they do not solve them in the same way.* The problem-solving process must standardize the steps that are taken to ensure not merely that they are effective, but also that everyone is doing the same necessary things. In this fashion there will be far better cooperation, more effective collaboration, and less wasted effort. The problem-solving process must be adopted by all stakeholders in order for it to be effective.

2. *Individuals resist a single systematic problem-solving method because they think it inhibits creativity or is too complex to follow.* The problem-solving process you adopt must be simple and fully understood by everyone involved, and the benefits of following the process must be appreciated. Otherwise, it will be avoided by some and resisted by others.

3. *Some organizations solve the wrong problem.* When they have solved a problem, often at considerable expense and after great difficulty, nobody cares. Or they discover that more important problems surface or that the problem they thought they solved wasn't solved at all. The problem-solving method should include a step that determines which problem the problem-solving team should tackle so that if and when they are successful, the organization benefits because the most important problem was solved.

4. *Sometimes the problem selected is too difficult for the team to solve at that time using the available resources.* It is critical to ensure that appropriate resources exist to address the problem and that the organization knows how to solve the problem. If these requirements cannot be met, the solution plan should not be accepted, since it will waste resources and is ultimately impossible.

5. *Most organizations define problems in a way that limits the number of possible solutions.* The problem should be defined (or redefined) in a fashion that permits a maximum number of possible solutions.

6. *Nearly all problem-solving processes include a step to determine only one root cause of the problem rather than multiple root causes.* But complex, recurring organizational problems rarely have a single, root cause, so removing just one will seldom resolves the issue. It is important to identify as many of a problem's causes as possible.

7. *The problem-solving process permits old, ineffective solutions to be tried again.* Creativity is essential to developing new and effective solutions to problems. Most problem-solving approaches emphasize the goal of generating innovative solutions, but they don't sufficiently stress the use of tools and practices to enhance creativity. The result is that new solutions still contain aspects of the old problem. The problem-solving process must include techniques that enhance the chances of developing a creative solution.

8. *Sometimes the solution introduces new complications.* The problem-solving process must include a step that forces the team to consider what impact the proposed solution will have on other processes and other business concerns.

9. *The problem-solving team stops before achieving buy-in from the management for implementation of the solution.* Nearly all problem-solving processes that organizations employ do not require the implementation of the solution. Those processes stop at making a recommendation for improvements to the organization; they do not demand that the appropriate managers who have the authority to implement the changes be persuaded to do so. The problem-solving process you adopt must include identifying who the

decision makers are and presenting to them a persuasive argument to implement the solution.

10. *The problem-solving team fails to carry out follow-up activities to determine whether the problem was and remains solved.* To have an effective process, follow-up must be planned and practiced or this step (and to some extent, the entire process) is meaningless. Simply put, there are no immediate consequences of not solving problems in most organizations. While everyone understands the benefits of addressing problems, organizations do not typically hold individuals accountable for identifying and resolving persistent problems, and therefore addressing them is often given only partial priority. The problem-solving process you adopt should include steps to create personal responsibility for the resolution of persistent problems.

In the seven-step problem-solving process that follows, I offer ways to avoid and overcome these challenges.

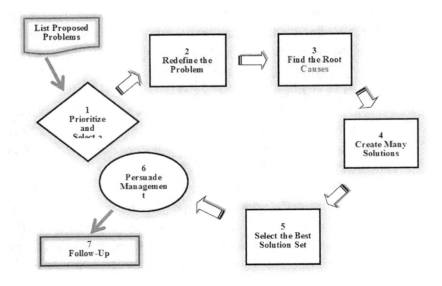

3. The Seven-Step Problem-Solving Process

Preliminary Activities—List Proposed Problems

In this subchapter we will discover how to identify persistent problems that inhibit an organization's ability to achieve its business objectives and how to differentiate these long-standing issues from sudden problems which can be solved more easily. The goal of this preliminary stage is to develop a list of "candidate" problems from which the best one to be solved can be selected. The outcome of this stage will be a list provided to the problem-solving team for Step One activities.

In many cases, the list of candidate problems may be short and choosing which one to address seems obvious. Examples of obvious problems that merit immediate attention are unexpected violations of regulatory rules or laws, sudden loss of a major customer or essential supplier, a startling accident causing death or injury, and sudden catastrophic failure of a product that is critical to the business. These problems are obvious and when one of them occurs it should be dealt with immediately. In these cases no selection is necessary. But these problems are not *persistent*.

Persistent problems are ones that have existed for a long time and have proven to be unresponsive to previous attempts to solve them. Examples of persistent problems are low employee morale, reduced productivity, inability to hire replacements for retiring employees, and gradual reduction in business metrics such as stock prices, profits, and cash flow. When the organization has unsuccessfully tried to solve stubborn problems that have not been resolved with simpler techniques, a more systematic approach is required, and this includes making a more subtle differentiation of the candidate problems. A systematic approach means creating a comprehensive list of candidate recurring organizational problems and determining which one is the best candidate for the problem-solving team to solve first.

These preliminary activities may be performed by management or by a problem-solving team selected by management. Problem-solving teams are often created to solve a specific recurring organizational problem that management feels prevents the organization from achieving its objectives. In that case, the team need not develop a large list of candidate problems to be solved— management effectively performs this preparatory activity before the problem-solving team is assigned its task. Whether management or the problem-solving team identifies those candidate problems that should be considered, developing the list ought to follow a systematic process like the one I have described in this subchapter.

In listing candidate problems, the team—or managers—can use any format they find useful to describe the problems. Since the problems will be redefined in Step Two, the list of candidate problems need not be precise in the preliminary stage. Examples of complaints such as "Employees feel they are not treated fairly," "We don't have the tools we need to do our jobs," and "We have a lack of training" are sufficient at this stage. Any phrasing that captures the importance of the concept is fine.

Whining Session

In my consulting practice, when I am asked to assist an organization in solving problems, I have the organization assemble a team of problem solvers and I begin by holding a "whining session." I encourage the team to list any and all of the problems that annoy or worry them about their current jobs, the places that they physically work, and the organization. I find that they have many issues on their minds but they often need some assistance in creating a comprehensive list of problems. In this fashion I have been successful in many organizations in developing a list of candidate problems quickly and with a minimum amount of effort.

There are many other approaches to surfacing those problems that prevent an organization from meeting its objectives effectively. These other methods usually require more time to apply than the "whining session" I ordinarily employ, but they actually provide greater confidence that the list of candidate problems is comprehensive. The problem-solving team or managers may wish to experiment with other methods for creating a preliminary list and determine which one works best for their particular environment. These are a few of the more popular techniques:

- *Brainstorming*
- *Third-Party Audits*
- *Voice of the Customer*
- *Benchmarking*
- *Checklists*
- *Identify Project Risk*
- *Identify Potential Product and Process Failures*
- *Operational Excellence*

Brainstorming

The most common approach to determining what is wrong with an organization is to assemble a group of people who are experiencing difficulties in performing their jobs and ask them to develop a list of problems. The technique often used for this task is "brainstorming." There are three considerations that must be incorporated into brainstorming if it is to be effective. (Brainstorming is useful for the wide identification of problems as in the preparatory stage discussed here, and it also is useful in identifying which problem should be resolved first, discussed in the next subchapter on Step One).

First of all, the experts assembled to perform the brainstorming must in fact be experts—that is, people with experience, not merely observers. Newly minted MBAs are not as useful in identifying what's wrong with an organization as blue-collar workers who are actually experiencing the problems! The brainstorming team must include people representing *all* levels of management. While senior executives have a clearer vision of what's wrong with the business situation of the organization, the shop floor workers have the best perspective of what's wrong with the daily operational processes. Also, the team should include people representing a large cross section of the organization's functions so the candidate problems will represent diverse perspectives. Manufacturing will identify different problems than procurement, and marketing will experience still different issues.

Second, in problem identification, the brainstorming activity includes an additional step that most brainstorming sessions do not include. We use the term "brainstorming" to refer to having a group of people think up a lot of ideas. The term was popularized by Alex Faickney Osborn in the 1953 book *Applied Imagination*. Osborn proposed that there be two parts to any group brainstorming session. The participants start by generating all the ideas they can on the topic at hand, before evaluating each idea independently to determine which ideas are the best. Accordingly, in determining what's wrong with an organization, the team should develop as long a list as possible of potential problems and then assess each idea to determine which is in most need of a solution.

Third, brainstorming candidate problems to be resolved may be much more difficult than it appears. While every organization has people who are constantly complaining, their complaints do not often surface problems of which the solution would greatly improve the overall operation of the organization. Accordingly, it is wise to incorporate some more rigorous methods to identify organizational problems, such as those listed below.

Third-Party Audits

Recurring problems would all be solved in any organization if they were easy to identify and easy to solve. The fact that problems don't get permanently resolved suggests that the people who are involved in the processes that contain the problems may be too close to them to see them clearly—they cannot see the forest for the trees. Accordingly, having someone outside the business process assess the process for possible issues may result in surfacing problems that otherwise are overlooked. Third-party audits conducted by individuals outside the organization will help provide a fresh perspective on what others are too close to see and are recommended in those situations.

Voice of the Customer

Most organizations know what to provide their customers. Product development processes include sophisticated techniques for determining what customers really like and don't like and to what extent this preference actually matters to them. If your organization has formal customer surveys or "Voice of the Customer" practices, the problem-solving team should consult those sources before creating its own list of potential problems.

A simple and often-used means for determining what customers think is to perform customer surveys and to collect and examine customer complaints.

Customer complaints, however, are a poor source for organizational and product problems since most customers do not complain officially about their experiences—if they don't like what you do for them they more often merely move on to another supplier or suffer in silence. Many organizations have effective survey techniques that do draw out customer feedback on products and services and their feelings about the way they are treated by the organization.

Benchmarking

Benchmarking has become a trusted method for identifying what an organization needs to do to improve its operational processes, products, and services. The technique consists of identifying a benchmarking partner—an organization that does similar business extremely well— and then determining how that organization might be emulated. Some professional associations such as the Software Engineering Institute, the American Society for Quality, and the Product Development Management Association collect and publish best industry practices, which serve as accessible and functional benchmarking tools. If your company is engaged in benchmarking practices, it would be wise for the problem-solving team to consult those who have participated in benchmarking before developing a list of potential problems.

Waste ("Muda") Checklist

If you have a list of things that should be done or standards to be achieved, it should be incorporated into brainstorming sessions to help identify organizational problems. One of the most powerful checklists is the one developed by the Toyota Production System in Japan to identify types of waste (or *muda*). In its current form as shown below, it consists of eight items, each of which can be employed to reveal problems in the organization. Simply have the team brainstorm each area and you will be surprised how many problems are surfaced that might otherwise be overlooked.

1. Waste resulting from overproduction
2. Waste from unnecessary process steps
3. Inventory waste
4. Inefficient transportation time and expenses
5. Waste from unnecessary motion
6. Wasted time from unnecessary waiting
7. Defects
8. Waste from unused employee talent

Identify Project Risk (5 X 5 Matrix)

Project management is an important skill that many organizations have recognized by implementing both internal and external training programs. Project management training programs nearly always include an emphasis on identifying and managing project risks—things that can go wrong and therefore cause the project to fail to fulfill its project goals. Anything that may cause the project to deviate from its plan is defined as a risk and the project management industry has developed some powerful techniques for seeking out and mitigating those risks. If your organization includes a project management office or has standardized project management practices, consult them for potential risks before embarking on brainstorming exercises aimed at identifying problems. One popular and powerful project risk management tool is the Risk Assessment Matrix, or "Five by Five" Matrix. The Risk Assessment Matrix is described in Tom Kendrick's 2009 book *Identifying and Managing Project Risk.*

Failure Modes and Effects Analysis (FMEA)

One of the most powerful practices developed by organizations to spot potential problems with products and services is the FMEA, or Failure Modes and Effects Analysis. This is a set of questions that guides the group to identify actual or potential failures in a concept, design, process, or service, and to determine whether and how to take action about the failures. Additionally, there is substantial literature on the topic of how to surface problems, including the application of statistical and probability tools to new product development and process improvement. If your organization possesses experts in FMEA, one or some of them should be included on the problem-solving team or at least in the brainstorming sessions that identify potential problems.

Operational Excellence

Operational excellence includes many management initiatives that organizations have adopted including Six Sigma, Total Quality Management, Lean Manufacturing or Lean Operations, and Design for Excellence. Every one of these initiatives incorporates powerful processes for detecting potential problems, risks, and opportunities. If your organization is currently engaged in one or more of these initiatives, it would benefit your problem-solving team to include what they have learned in the problem-identification process.

Summary of Actions Necessary in the Preliminary Actions Stage

There is only one action required in the preliminary stage: develop a comprehensive list of candidate problems for the problem-solving team or management to consider in Step One. This may be accomplished by employing the "whining session" or by one of the more systematic methods mentioned above, if management or the team needs to increase their confidence in its list.

Step One—Prioritize and Select a Problem

Step One is aimed at ensuring that the people working on solving the problem have a thorough and accurate understanding of why this problem was selected. In this subchapter we will discover how to choose one problem from the list of candidate problems. While several powerful and effective selection techniques and tools exist, we explore one that is easy to implement and has been shown to be effective. This selection technique is the BCG Matrix and we will demonstrate how to employ it to determine the one candidate problem the solution of which should be sought first.

Sometimes management selects the problem then assigns it a problem-solving team. In this instance, the priority of this problem must be determined by management and relayed to the team.

Determining which problem to solve involves prioritization. By analogy, there is always a long list of necessary activities that managers and employees must perform *right now!* But, there are never enough resources and never enough time to perform them all simultaneously, so intelligent businesses prioritize the activities and work on the most important ones first. The problem-solving team must operate in the same way, ensuring that the problem they solve is both feasible and important to the organization before they undertake it.

There are two considerations for selecting a problem to solve. First, the problem must be solvable—if we do not have the resources and the technical skills necessary to solve the problem, attempting to do so will only frustrate us. Of course, we seldom know in advance whether a problem is solvable, but there are some problems that we know we cannot solve, and it is foolish to attempt them. For example, if you believe your workforce lacks commitment to your company's objectives and you honestly believe that the reason is that "kids today are not taught to be responsible," you shouldn't try to solve this problem. The organization will have a hard time educating all young people entering the workforce to be more responsible. It will be more productive for you to focus on solving the parts of the problem you can successfully influence, such as re-training those young people you hire.

The second consideration for selecting a problem to solve is that the problem must be significant. If you spend a lot of time, money, and energy solving a problem only to learn it really doesn't matter to the company, you will be left wondering why you should bother the next time you are asked to solve a problem.

There are many powerful techniques for prioritizing items on a list, including prioritizing the potential problems developed in the pre-problem-solving, whining session. A good starting place to explore these techniques is the Internet. Some additional prioritization techniques that can be researched are these:

- BCG Matrix
- Pair-Wise Comparison
- Weighted Matrix
- Pugh Selection Technique

- Analytic Hierarchy Process (AHP)
- Failure Modes and Effects Analysis (FMEA)

I have found that most problem-solving teams do not have the time to apply most of these techniques, although they are all powerful and effective when utilized. An online search will turn up many books and articles on these techniques. The technique that works best, in my experience, is the BCG Matrix because it is the simplest and easiest to perform.

BCG (Silver Bullet) Matrix

The Boston Consulting Group (BCG) developed a matrix for comparing products with the market's need for them. The BCG Matrix has been used widely with great success by businesses for over thirty years. It has been adapted for other situations and used for other purposes, sometimes with similarly notable success. The version of the BCG chart I recommend illustrates the relationship between our ability to solve problems and the potential to solve them.

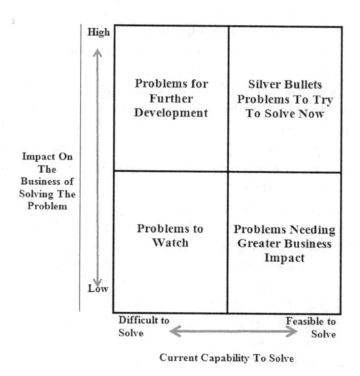

We should always consider both the feasibility of solving the problem (the horizontal axis on the chart) and the impact that solving the problem will have on our business (the vertical axis) before we select any problem to be solved. Some problems are easier to solve and will have a greater impact when they are addressed. These are the "Silver Bullets" on the chart, and clearly, we want to work on those problems.

The process of employing this BCG Matrix tool to select a problem from the list of candidate problems consists of determining the relative importance and feasibility of each candidate problem and then plotting them on the BCG Matrix chart. We do this by first dividing the entire list into two parts—those that are relatively more important in one group and those that are relatively less important in the other. In practice, it is imperative that we resist the urge to define everything as "equally very important," and place exactly one-half in each group. Next, we divide the entire list into two groups of equal halves—those that are relatively more feasible than the other half and those that are relatively less feasible. We can then plot the candidate problems on the BCG Matrix.

Those candidate problems that fall in the Silver Bullet quadrant are the ones we should try to solve first. Ordinarily, there will be a small number in this quadrant, but it is often more than one. We must then determine the relative importance and feasibility of the Silver Bullet problems. We can plot them on another BCG Matrix to determine which single problem should be selected to be solved first, but it is often possible to arbitrarily select one Silver Bullet problem to start with and return to the others as soon as the problem-solving team is completed with the first one. Or, we may decide to perform a quantitative comparison of all the candidate problems that fall in the Silver Bullet quadrant.

Generally, it is unnecessary to apply quantitative measures to compare the feasibility and importance of solving every one of the candidate problems, but it is a good idea to develop comparative metrics for those that fall in the Silver Bullet quadrant. Such metrics should include accessible measures of the importance and feasibility of the solution of the candidate problem. For example, we might determine what amount of money is lost each year until we solve each of the Silver Bullet candidate problems, and we could use that to determine the one that would result in the greatest savings. And we might determine how long and what resources it will take to solve each of the Silver Bullet candidate problems, and we could use that to determine the one that is least costly to solve. While these metrics are not absolutely essential at this stage of the problem-solving process, they will provide a better basis for redefining the problem in Step Two and will be extremely useful in persuading management to implement the recommended solutions in Step Six.

After we have found and solved the easier-to-address and more important problems (the Silver Bullets), we will want to find and solve the ones that did not fall in the Silver Bullet quadrant. These will be harder to solve, less important, or both.

Here is an example of how the BCG Matrix might be used to prioritize some projects that are being considered. Imagine that the team has uncovered eighteen possible problems to be solved:

1. Senior people are retiring, creating an intellectual capital drain.
2. The organization can't replace departing people—there aren't enough talented people to replace them.
3. The organization acquired another company and the people in the acquired firm don't want to follow our processes.
4. Management directs employees to do things but fails to provide the authority and resources necessary to accomplish them.
5. Decisions by management and authorizations to proceed take too long.
6. Supplier delivers poor quality components.
7. We have good profits but poor cash flow so we can't pay current expenses.
8. Morale is low.
9. Trust is low.
10. We have dysfunctional teams.
11. Management won't implement solutions recommended by the QA department.
12. Our organization has rigid silos and there is little inter-departmental cooperation.
13. Management promises things that aren't feasible to deliver.
14. People feel stagnated in jobs—see no place to go.
15. New hires have poor work ethics and habits.

16. People don't accept accountability for their responsibilities.
17. There is little attention to results.
18. There are not enough resources to do everything we are expected to do.

The problem-solving team will then have to prioritize these problems to identify the one that must be worked on first. They begin by dividing the list of eighteen candidate problems into two groups, placing an *I* for relatively more important next to exactly one-half of the candidates, and an *L* for relatively less important next to the other half. There must be nine *I*'s and nine *L*'s.

Next, the problem-solving team divides the list into two equal halves, considering the feasibility of the organization to solve the problem. Given the resources we have, the capability of the staff, and the nature of the problem to be solved, which ones are more likely to be solved and which ones aren't? The team places an *F* next to those candidate problems that are relatively more feasible, that is, easier to solve than the other half, and a *D* next to those that are relatively more difficult, that is, harder to solve. Once again, there must be exactly nine of each of these labels.

While your organization will evaluate these factors differently than any other organization will for the given set of candidate problems, imagine that the team has assigned the following assessments to the eighteen problems listed:

Problem ID	Problem	Importance	Feasibility
(1)	Senior people are retiring	I	D
(2)	Can't replace departing people	I	F
(3)	Acquired company doesn't practice our policies	L	F
(4)	Management fails to give authority and resources	I	D
(5)	Decisions take too long	L	F
(6)	Supplier delivers poor quality components	I	D
(7)	Poor cash flow	I	D

(8)	Low morale	L	F
(9)	Lack of trust	I	F
(10)	Dysfunctional teams	L	F
(11)	QA recommendations not adopted	L	D
(12)	Lack inter-department cooperation	L	D
(13)	Management over-promises	L	D
(14)	Lack visible career paths	L	F
(15)	New hires have poor work practices	I	D
(16)	Lack accountability	L	F
(17)	No focus on results	I	F
(18)	Not enough resources	I	D

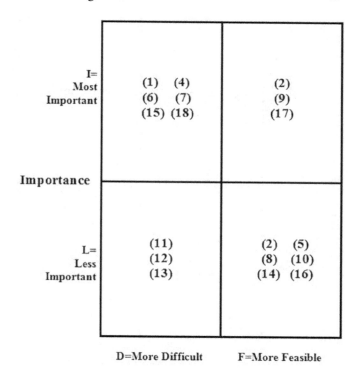

D=More Difficult   F=More Feasible

Feasibility

In this example, three candidate problems emerged in the "Silver Bullet" quadrant. These, according to the assessment made by the problem-solving team in this example, are the ones that should be worked on first. The team may want to perform the BCG assessment on these three as well or merely determine a way that all three can be worked on simultaneously, if that is possible. The team may seek to develop a process for replacing retiring employees, developing better trust among team members, and getting employees to better focus on results as their top priorities. Or the problem-solving team may elect to try to solve only one of these silver bullet problems.

I have developed a "rule of thumb" for interpreting the BCG chart after a prioritizing exercise. Here is how I interpret each of the quadrants ("window panes") in the chart:

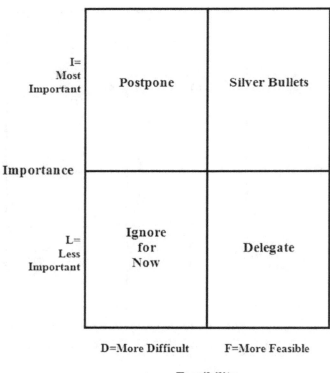

Here is my logic for this "rule of thumb":

- Those candidate problems that fall into the upper right-hand quadrant are the "silver bullets" and should receive highest attention as early as possible.
- Those in the upper left-hand quadrant should be delayed until the team is finished with the silver bullets and can devote time to them. Postponing isn't ignoring the problems—it is scheduling the problem-solving attention for a later time.
- Those candidates that fall into the lower right-hand quadrant might best be delegated to someone else. Since they are easier to do, it is more likely someone else can do them well, and since they are less important if they are not done perfectly there will be less impact on the overall organization's objectives than if other problems were poorly resolved.
- And finally, if the candidates fall into the lower left-hand quadrant, they should be ignored until the other ones are dealt with: these problems are both difficult and less important. If management insists that they be addressed, the problem-solving team may need to ask management to make the job easier by providing additional resources or exchanging one of these candidates with one that has been ranked more important.

Summary of Actions Necessary in Step One—Prioritize and Select a Problem to Solve

1. Consider all of the candidate problems.
2. Determine the feasibility of solving each candidate problem.
3. Establish the importance of solving the problem to the organization.
4. Prioritize the candidate problems using a tool such as the BCG Matrix.
5. Select the one problem that the team believes to be both feasible and important to solve.
6. If quantitative metrics were developed to determine the feasibility and the importance of solving the selected problem, provide them for Step Two, Redefine the Problem. These metrics will also be used in Step 6, Persuade Management to Implement the Solutions.

Step Two—Redefine the Problem

In this subchapter we learn how to redefine the problem in a fashion that increases our chances of solving the problem and provides metrics that can be used to measure our progress toward solving the problem during the process as well as prove the problem has been solved when it has (at the end of the problem-solving process).

In this step, we ensure that the selected problem is defined in terms of *the gap between what we'd like to have happen and what is actually happening.* If necessary, we redefine the problem to meet this standard. We also quantify the gap—we use numbers to describe it. This type of definition increases the opportunities to solve the problem. It also supports the next step in the process, which seeks to discover root causes of the problem. In addition, the quantifying of the gap supports the follow-up stage (Step Seven, discussed later), since it gives us a basis for measuring the results of our efforts and for demonstrating that we have solved the problem. Examples of defining a problem in terms of a gap are provided in the chart below in this subchapter.

Gap Definition

For purposes of the preparation stage and Step One, it is sufficient to generally name or describe problems. In this Step Two we generate a specific definition of the problem so that we all understand to what we refer. This also helps to make clear the nature and scope of the problem.

Most people define a problem as the absence of their "pet solution"—the one that jumps to mind as soon as a person considers a problem. In nearly all cases, the pet solution has been tried before without success or is so obvious that it would already have been tried if it would work.

There is a deeper issue, however. When we define any problem as the absence of a particular solution, there is really *only one way to solve that problem* as defined: you must provide the solution that is missing. Defining a problem in this manner limits our understanding of the problem and our access to the full range of solutions to eliminate the problem, including the best solutions. By redefining the problem as the gap between the ideal and the current situation, we increase the possible solutions from one (the pet solution) to many. Since we are not constrained to only one solution when the problem is redefined as the gap, we have the opportunity to look for many solutions, as we explore later in the subchapter for Step Four.

Consider this example. I asked a manager what problem her organization was experiencing. She said, "We don't have enough training." What she meant was, "I think we need a certain amount of training and we don't have that much so I think our problem is that we need more training." Actually, she's defining her problem as the lack of training, which she believes is the source of her problem. Her pet solution is more training. She believes more training will make her organization better able to meet its obligations.

In all likelihood, however, a better statement of the problem would indicate that the organization does not have enough people with the knowledge and skills to perform all of their assigned jobs. Providing more training as the manager advocates might be one solution, but it might be insufficient by itself or it might not be the best solution. Among the best solutions might be the following: (a) hiring people who already have the necessary skills and knowledge; (b) outsourcing the jobs to another organization better staffed to fulfill the obligations; (c) reducing the obligations of the organization so the skills and knowledge the current employees possess may be sufficient; or (d) a combination of all of these or other possible solutions. By improperly defining her problem as the absence of training, she will miss the opportunity to consider and try these other possible solutions. In this case, lack of training is certainly a possible cause of her problem but defining her problem as a gap between what she would like to have and what she has introduces more possible causes and opens opportunities for discovering a greater number of solutions.

In the table below are four common expressions that define problems in terms of what's missing. Although the typical statements in this table do express issues that are indeed frustrating to the organization's management and workforce, they are solvable only by providing what the statement says is missing. And that may not be—and usually is not—the best solution. In this table I have *speculated* in order to show what actual situation might lead someone to make a typical statement.

In these cases, the probability of finding a permanent solution is increased if we redefine the problem as a gap between what we'd like to have happen and what is actually happening and if we also quantify that gap. Here are some examples of how we might redefine the four typical statements to increase the opportunities for solving them. (In the first and third columns, the bracketed information describes some possible solutions that flow from each particular definition shown.)

	Typical Statement	A Possible Situation	The Problem Redefined as a Gap
a.	We don't have enough training [can only be solved by providing more training].	100 percent of our engineers need to be level 3, but 85 percent of our engineers are level 1 and level 2.	To perform our current work load, we need to acquire 85 percent more Level 3 engineers [by training, hiring, or by lowering the requirements].
b.	We can't replace retiring people [can only be solved by replacing retiring people].	We need 1,000 skilled employees to achieve our current corporate goals. We expect to lose 300 of our current work force in the next three years.	To close the staffing gap, we must acquire 300 more skilled workers than we have during the next three years [by hiring, training current employees, or by an acquisition, or by lowering the requirements].
c.	We need more customers [can only be solved by getting more customers].	The ideal situation is profits of $1 million per year or better. Our profits are down by 25 percent and at current product margins we would need to sell 10 million more units next year.	We need to increase profits by $250,000 or more next year [by increasing the number of customers, increasing the margin on each unit, or by opening different markets and offering different products].
d.	Employee morale is low [could only be solved by raising morale— and it's not clear how we would know it's been raised if it were].	The ideal situation is for 100 percent of our employees to report a 4 or 5 (highest) satisfaction rating each year on the employee satisfaction survey. But last year only 10 percent of our employees reported 4s and 5s.	We need to have 90 percent of our employees raise their satisfaction ratings from 3 or lower to 4s and 5s [by discovering why they are giving lower ratings and overcoming their objections].

In my workshops I have discovered that many people have trouble identifying the ideal situation and therefore are unable to redefine their problems as gaps between what they would like to have and what they actually have. I have found that it takes practice to develop the skill to see an ideal situation in the problems that confront them. Our society places so much emphasis on finding solutions immediately that many of us lack the ability to work our way to the best possible solution. One manager I know had a sign, which I now believe to be inappropriate, in his office that said this:

Are you here with a solution to the problem, or are you part of it?

As children we are taught to try to think of a solution to a problem before we present the problem. But there is an obvious difficulty with doing that. In the case of complex, organizational problems, there are no simple and obvious solutions. If the problem were easy to solve, it would have already been solved! Since it hasn't been solved, asking individuals to generate solutions to the problems they encounter before they've explored and analyzed them thoroughly will result in them seeing the obvious solutions that have already been tried— and failed. If we want to resolve persistent organizational problems we must discard the directive to "tell me about a problem only if you've thought up a solution to it."

Thus, what I'm proposing here is that we change the way people within organizations, including the managers, think about problems. Personally, I believe that the job of managers is to help their employees to identify problems and to help them develop permanent solutions to their problems.

Summary of Actions Necessary in Step Two—Redefine the Problem

1. Identify the ideal situation—what would the organization be like if the problem were permanently solved. Metrics should be used to describe the ideal situation.

2. Determine the current situation in the same metrics.
3. Compute the difference between the ideal and the current (actual) situation.
4. Redefine the problem as this gap which must be closed.
5. Provide these metrics and the redefined problem to Step Three—Find the Root Causes. The metrics will also be used in Step Six—Persuade Management to Implement the Solutions.

Step Three—Find the Root Causes

Root Cause Analysis

Here we will examine why finding the root causes is essential, then we will cover some specific activities for determining root causes.

We can identify root causes by the fact that when they are eliminated, the stubborn problem goes away. Note that we are looking in this step to find root causes (plural) rather than a root cause (singular). Complex organizational problems are due to the interactions of several simultaneous forces. We will not find a single root cause to *any* of the persistent organizational problems we are trying to solve. So we must look for that entire *set* of causes, the elimination of which would permanently solve the problem.

"Eliminating root causes" means simultaneously removing all of the influences that are causing the main problem to exist. It is simply a matter of removing all of *the causes of a result* to the degree necessary to ensure that the *result no longer exists*. For example, consider a light bulb. When it is emitting light we know that it is receiving electricity. We can say the electricity is a root cause of an otherwise functional light bulb's emitting light. If we stop the electricity reaching the bulb, then the bulb will stop emitting light—the influence of the electricity to cause the bulb to emit light has been eliminate or removed.

But if our problem is not that the bulb is emitting light, but rather that it is not, we can say one cause of this problem is that the bulb is not receiving electricity. In this case, a root cause of an otherwise functional bulb's failing to emit light is that no electricity is being received by it. But, if we now provide electricity to the bulb, the bulb will emit light so we can say that turning on the electricity to the light bulb eliminates or removes the root cause of the bulb failing to emit light. Of course, other causes may exist for a bulb failing to emit light—the bulb may be broken, burned out, or not screwed tightly into the socket. When we eliminate or remove a single root cause by providing electricity, we must also ensure we eliminate all the other root causes, or we will not remove the main problem, failure to emit light.

The practice of seeking the root causes of a difficult organizational problem is straightforward and there are some powerful tools that can assist the problem-solving team in finding them. This step involves four parts:

first, identifying possible causes with recommended teamwork tools; second, using a team voting process to select the greatest contributing cause; third, identifying additional causes, and fourth, ensuring the statement of the root causes include what will be needed to solve the problem later in the process.

The first task in seeking the root causes involves identifying possible causes of the problem as it has been defined (that is, as the gap between the ideal and the current situations). This task is best performed by brainstorming a list and also using some specialized but simple analytical tools for identifying other causes that might not be discovered by simple brainstorming alone. The brainstorming component can be performed simply and fairly quickly. Merely asking a group of intelligent people to brainstorm all possible causes of the problem will result in a long list of possible causes.

Using some additional analytical tools will help generate even more potential causes and will help reveal relationships among causes. The tools will also help show which causes are more significant. These tools do not automatically generate one "correct" answer. Instead, they assist a group of intelligent people in determining the possible causes of the problem. Here I will describe four powerful analytical techniques briefly, and then I will discuss in detail an especially powerful tool that utilizes a diagram. For those unfamiliar with these named techniques, other books or Internet resources describe these in more detail. Anderson and Fagerhaug's *Root Cause Analysis: Simplified Tools and Techniques* is an excellent source for these and other tools.

- *Drill Down.* This is a technique of breaking the problem down into components. While this is not always possible, the breakdown permits a closer, more detailed inspection of the impact of various influences leading to a problem. Everyone has experience doing this. Imagine your car won't start, for example. You consider some of the components of the car that may have failed, causing the car to not start. First, you check to see if the lights work. If they do not, you know the battery is dead. If the lights work, you check to see if the gas tank indicator shows you are out of gas. If you have enough gas, you may turn the key again to see if the starter motor is trying to engage. If it is not engaging when it has power applied to it, you have determined the starter motor is malfunctioning. If it is engaging but the engine still won't work, you suspect there may be no gas getting to the engine—possibly your gas pump isn't working. This simple process can be more complicated for organizational problems, but it is in principle the same. By drilling down you consider the components to gain a more detailed perspective of what might be causing the problem.

- *Fault Tree Analysis.* This is a graphic approach to breaking the problem's potential causes into those components, events, or factors that might have caused the problem. A diagram is drawn showing the relationships between the contributing influences and in what way they contribute to the problem. The probability of each contributing element occurring is then assigned and its statistical impact on the problem is illustrated. The technique forces the problem-solving team to consider relationships between causes and often helps surface causes that would otherwise have been missed. Commercial software programs are available to guide teams and individuals in creating the diagrams, calculating the probabilities, and identifying the relationships. Sources for free software to complete these tasks can be found on the Internet.

- *Five Why's.* This is a technique that has been used in quality improvement programs. The problem-solving team asks "Why did this problem happen?" When a possible answer is identified, the team asks "Why did this cause happen?" The process is repeated— the title of the technique suggests that the team repeat this process four more times for each possible cause of the main problem. But in practice, most teams continue asking "why" until they feel they have exhausted all possible causes and have settled on one cause that is the earliest contributor to the problem. When this method is repeated by a different team or the same team at a different time, other causes are surfaced that are, at that time, considered to be the greatest contributor to the problem. In this fashion, several candidates for the set of root causes are identified.

- *So What?* This is merely a technique of asking "So what?" about all possible causes. The problem-solving team begins by identifying a list of possible causes by some other means, and then for each one of these possible causes asks "So what?" That is, "Does it matter?"

And, "If so, why?" In this way the team explores the relationship of each possible cause to its consequences and in that fashion determines those causes which have most likely triggered the main problem to occur. The team often surfaces possible causes they otherwise would not have considered.

Ishikawa ("Fishbone") Diagram

The Ishikawa Diagram was invented by Kaoru Ishikawa, a Japanese industrial engineer, and was first published in 1968. It is often called the Fishbone Diagram because of its appearance when it is drawn as a graphic. It has also been called the Cause and Effects Diagram. Whatever its name, it is a tool that can be used to assist the problem-solving team to discover possible causes of the main problem.

The Ishikawa Diagram is used by the problem-solving team to assist them in making a list of possible causes of the main problem. The process begins with the drawing of the following diagram on a flip chart or white board:

The problem is written succinctly in the "head" of the diagram and the six "ribs" of the fishbone are each labeled according to one of the following schemes, M's, P's, or S's.

Six M's	Six P's	Six S's
Manpower	People	Skills
Material	Parts	Supplies
Methods	Procedures	Specifications
Machine	Process	System
Measure	Performance	Standards
Milieu (Environment)	Place	Surroundings

The categories are not sacred. The ribs of the fishbone may be labeled with any checklist that makes sense to the problem-solving team, and there may be more or less than six topics. The topics give the team a checklist of areas to suggest potential causes. In my workshops, if there is not a reason to use another set of labels, I ordinarily use the Six P's because I find they are the most recognizable by my client's team members.

We may then populate the labeled ribs of the fishbone graphic with brainstorming ideas that reflect possible causes of the problem. This is what an abbreviated one would look like for the example we've chosen:

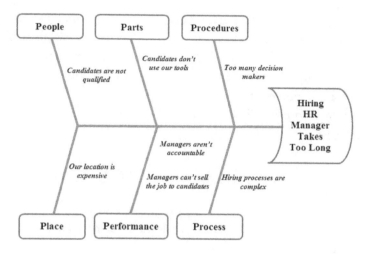

The results of the Ishikawa Diagram analysis can be added to or merged with the possible causes generated by the various brainstorming or analytical process tools.

The second task in this part of Step Three is to reach a team consensus on which one potential cause is the single largest contributor to the main problem. This is most effectively accomplished by a process of multiple voting.

Multi-Voting

Using an example where there are eighteen items on the list of potential causes and one must be chosen as the greatest contributing cause:

1. Regardless of the number of participants, assign each participant one third as many votes as there are things to prioritize—in our example, each participant has six votes (one third of eighteen). Round up or down if the dividend is not a whole number.
2. Have everyone cast their votes on the question presented. Voters can distribute their votes however they see fit, casting all (six) votes for one item, or distributing their votes among multiple items, such as two to one item, three to another, and one to yet another item.
3. Remove those items receiving few votes from further multi-voting consideration.
4. Repeat the multi-voting with the remaining items as necessary. If the first round produced six candidate causes, we would assign two votes for each person for the second round. If there are three for the third round, then we would assign only one vote for the third round, which would be the last, unless there is a tie, in which case a final round will be used to come to a consensus about which one cause is the single largest contributor to the main problem.

With the second part of Step Three accomplished, we must undertake the third part, which is to identify other causes that, together with the single greatest cause, comprise the entire set of root causes of the problem. The third activity of Step Three develops other root causes besides the single greatest cause already identified.

5. After the problem-solving team identifies the one primary cause, the team must ask the question, "If that cause is removed, what additional causes are there which individually or together still cause the main problem to occur?" They must then sort through this list and choose all additional causes that jointly form the set of causes that are the root causes.

It is important to notice that the additional causes considered need not have ever been identified in the brainstorming exercise using the Ishikawa Diagram. Many teams want to simply take the causes that received the second-most or third-most votes during the multi-voting, but this is not the point of the activity. Teams should perform this activity as described and specifically seek out causes that have not surfaced in any prior activities regarding this problem. After the team's careful consideration, any cause, regardless of how it was found, can be included in the final selection of additional causes. Ultimately, the team must identify which causes, together with the greatest contributing cause, constitute the set of root causes.

Here is an example. Suppose that the main issue is that management decisions take too long and we have defined the problem as a gap of five days. The ideal is every management decision must take one day or less, and we are currently measuring an average of six days for decisions to be made (five days longer than we consider ideal). Suppose that the problem-solving team determines that the one greatest contributing cause of the main problem is that there is not a published policy regarding how long managers should take to make a decision.[1] If we publish an appropriate policy, we eliminate this cause of the main problem. If that were the only cause of the problem, the problem would be immediately solved by merely publishing the policy.

But in this case the greatest contributing cause is not the *sole* root cause of the main problem. If we publish a policy, we probably will continue to experience delays in getting management to make decisions in one day or less. Even if we have a policy, we have no reason to believe managers will follow the new guidelines—if they have not followed other policies in the past, why would they follow this one? Sometimes managers fail to follow policies because they do not know about them, because they are not accountable to follow them, or because they are too busy to follow policies when they don't need to. We will have to make sure that all of the managers are aware of the new policy regarding decision-making time frames and we must ensure that there are real consequences for managers who do not follow the new policy. The complete set of root causes are all of the following:

1. No written policy regarding how long managers are supposed to take to make a decision exists.
2. Managers are not aware of all of the policies (including this new policy).
3. Managers are not held accountable for following policies (including this new policy).

35

It should be obvious that the problem-solving team would not have identified the last two of these as possible causes since, until they consider implementing a solution that removes the first cause (i.e., until they consider what will happen when the first cause is removed), they will not think to address what reaction that part of the solution will receive and what additional difficulties they may have after the first cause is eliminated.

The fourth and last activity in Step Three is to carefully prepare a statement of the root causes. The main problem has been redefined as the gap between the ideal and the current situation, and we have always attempted to include quantitative measures in this definition. We do this so we can measure progress toward solving the problem and so that we will be able to prove that the problem has been solved when the process is completed. Accordingly, we must ensure that the root causes, taken together, include the metrics necessary for us to show progress and demonstrate completion in the same way we do for the main problem.

Consider this example to illustrate how the root causes might include the quantitative metrics that redefined the main problem. Suppose the problem was redefined as, "We must hire 300 skilled workers over the next three years." And further suppose that we determined the root causes of this problem are: we do not have an effective acquisition program; candidates often do not accept the offers we make; and the salary we offer candidates is below the industry averages, so the candidates accept a competitor's offer rather than ours. We would need to do some research to identify quantitative measures for each of these root causes. By way of illustration, if we discover we are currently hiring twenty-five people per year we know we will have to increase this by seventy-five new hires per year. If we learn that the acceptance rate is only 33 percent, we know that we will have to increase the success of the offering process by 67 percent. If we learn that our company is offering candidates salaries 2,000 dollars per year below industry averages, we know the level of salary offer we need to achieve is 2,000 dollars more than we are offering. Our root causes, expressed in quantitative terms are:

1. Increase hiring levels by seventy-five skilled individuals per year.
2. Improve acceptance rate by 67 percent.
3. Increase annual salary offers by 2,000 dollars per new hire employee.

For those interested in learning more on this topic, there are other powerful methods for determining root causes including Kepner-Tregoe Problem Analysis and some software tools such as TapRooT. Information on these tools can be found online, although these methods are unnecessary when the process described here is followed.

Summary of Actions Necessary in Step Three—Find the Root Causes

1. Identify possible causes with recommended teamwork tools such as the Ishikawa Diagram.
2. Use a team process such as multi-voting to select the greatest contributing cause to the main problem.
3. Identify all additional causes that, taken together with the greatest contributing cause, constitute the complete set of root causes.
4. Prepare a statement of each of the root causes that includes quantitative measures that are consistent with the metrics used in the redefinition of the main problem as a gap between the ideal and current situation.
5. Provide the complete set of the root causes to Step Four—Produce Many Solutions.

Step Four—Produce Many Solutions

In this subchapter, we discover how to produce many possible solutions which will eliminate the root causes that were identified in Step Three. To accomplish this, we will define what we mean by the term "solution." Next we will discover how individuals find creative ideas, and then we will explore some proven techniques to enhance group creativity so that innovative approaches to removing the root causes can be considered in addition to any less creative solutions that have been tried before. We then conclude this subchapter by learning how the problem-solving team can apply the enhanced, creative techniques to develop many solutions that eliminate the root causes and thereby permanently remove the main problem.

So that the team has a common reference, we define "solution" as all the actions necessary to eliminate one or more root causes of the main problem. The "solution set" is the complete set of all actions necessary to remove all of the root causes that were identified in Step Three, which, when simultaneously taken, will permanently solve the main problem which we defined as a gap in Step Two. Because some of the solutions we develop in this Step Four will be farfetched and impractical, we will need to determine the practical and effective ones to implement, and that will be accomplished in the Step Five—Select the Best Solution Set.

The reason we need to determine many solutions is that persistent organizational problems are complex and will not be solved by simple means. As I have pointed out earlier, if the problem were simple and easy to solve, it would already have been solved! In order to solve complex recurring problems we need to develop innovative ideas that approach the problem in resourceful ways. The best way to accomplish this is to develop many solutions, some of which are significantly different from the obvious approaches that have been tried unsuccessfully in the past. Our solution set, i.e. all of the solutions we implement to solve the main problem, will probably include some ideas that were tried previously, but it will also include some new imaginative ones (the solution set will be identified in Step Five).

To resolve difficult, complex, and persistent organizational problems, we will need to apply innovative and creative thinking. We need to employ creativity-enhancing techniques to break out of the mental habits of applying what has been tried before but has not worked.

To understand the creative processes, we must first understand how the human mind works. There are two types of thinking that the mind practices: divergent and convergent.

Divergent thinking is developing alternatives, building and amplifying, and expanding previous ideas. It is "creativity" in that it generates new ideas or solutions. Edward de Bono has described this as "lateral thinking." The first part of brainstorming, where many ideas are generated, is an application of group divergent thinking.

Convergent thinking is the other type of thinking. It is selecting the best alternative, modifying each idea to make it compatible with the constraints, and assessing the relative value of all of the ideas. When we use the term "innovation" we are describing the development of practical applications of the ideas we developed in the divergent phase, and we are exercising convergent thinking. Divergent thinking that is not followed by convergent thinking to analyze, select, and tailor the ideas generated is a waste of time.

To experience how this sequence of divergent and then convergent thinking is how we solve problems, try to solve the puzzle below. As you do so, observe your thought processes. It is important to notice when you dream up all sorts of crazy ideas (divergent thinking) and then "try them on for size" (convergent thinking). When you find an idea that "makes sense," you feel you have solved the puzzle. One answer is on the end of Step Four subchapter.

Remove eight sticks to leave two squares:

The creative process of a group is the same as the creative process of individuals, namely, to "think up ideas" (divergent thinking) and then to "assess the effectiveness of the ideas" (convergent thinking). To enhance the creative solution process of the problem-solving team, it is necessary to apply techniques and tools that help the group first generate ideas and apply techniques and tools that aid the group in determining which of the ideas generated in the divergent thinking phase will be effective if they are implemented.

There is certainly no shortage of techniques for enhancing creativity but in my experience the two methods Brute Think and Honorable Thief and a more sophisticated version of the Honorable Thief known as TRIZ are the most approachable ones that are effective.

Many books have been published that describe creativity enhancement techniques. Certainly the most prolific writer on this topic is Edward de Bono, who has written dozens of books. His Six Hats and Lateral Thinking concepts are especially powerful, but you can obtain many ideas from his large library. Gerald Nadler and Iris Firstenberg are associates of mine and I respect their work on the subject of creativity enhancement. Gerald Nadler coauthored a book with Shozo Hibino on the subject entitled *Breakthrough Thinking*, and Iris Firstenberg has coauthored one with Moshe Rubinstein entitled *Patterns of Problem Solving*. The Internet is an excellent source for finding creativity-enhancing techniques.

Brute Think

This technique involves finding a random word and forcing a connection to the problem you are trying to solve. For example, if the solution you are seeking is to reduce the high turnover rate of your company's workforce, suppose you pick the random word "prison." On the surface, there is no connection between prisons and high turnover, but you let your team mull the word over and they might come up with these connections:

High security	Keeping employees in the firm at gun point	Locking up all the employees
Deflecting the reasons people want to leave	Trustees	Visits to prisoners by family members and friends
Menial tasks	License plates	Learning new trades
Putting prisoners to work	Using pay phones	Etc.

One company actually had this problem and used this word to force ideas about how to solve the high turnover rate of their telemarketing operators. From the brainstorming session they got the idea to use actual prisoners, worked out a deal with the warden of a local prison, and started using trustees for their boiler room operations. They haven't had much unpredicted turnover and their sales have improved. But most importantly, the prisoners and the community view what this company is doing as proactive assistance to the prisoners and it has received plenty of free publicity.

Note that the word that the problem-solving team selects need not be connected to the problem they are trying to solve. It is tempting to look for words that have obvious connections to your problem or to the most obvious solutions to it. But that is not the best use of Brute Think. Brute Think is best performed when the word selected is not obviously connected; in that case, you have to stretch to find connections and causing you to think "out of the box." It is precisely the far-fetched ideas that are most likely to produce a new and original way to view the problem and to come up with an innovative solution.

The Honorable Thief

The Honorable Thief is a benchmarking technique that consists of systematically finding other venues where a problem similar to yours has been solved, and then adapting one or more of the best solutions in order to solve your problem. It is called the Honorable Thief because it involves "stealing" successful ideas from one situation and applying them to another. This is a powerful technique, and for extremely difficult problems it may bring better results than some other techniques do. The technique is not as simple as it sounds, however, so where possible, it is best that the problem-solving team be guided by a leader with special skills or experience in this technique.

The Honorable Thief technique consists of the following steps:

1. Define your problem.
2. Brainstorm a large list of any organizations that have previously solved a problem like yours and describe the solution.
3. Review every solution on your list, identifying the major characteristics of the solution that contributed to its success.
4. Determine whether each solution's major characteristic applies to your problem.
5. Develop a list of possible solutions to your problem (I recommend seven to twelve) by selecting the best solutions that have worked on other problems or by crafting different solutions that incorporate characteristics that aided success in other contexts.

Here is an example of the Honorable Thief technique in action. A community college, seeking to reach out in its community, asked several local manufacturing firms what they needed most. The firms told the community college that their number one problem was recruiting entry-level machinists and metal workers. Because it is not the business of community colleges to assist companies in recruiting new employees, the community college representatives could not immediately recommend a solution. They knew how to provide training and education for entry-level employees once they were hired by companies, but they didn't know what the companies should do to recruit more candidates. A team was formed with representatives of the community college and some manufacturing firms. The team held a four-hour brainstorming session to generate new and creative ideas to improve entry-level employee recruiting. The team identified more than fifty organizations that had been successful in recruiting people in the past. This list included some obvious organizations such as the military and prestigious colleges. It also included far-fetched ideas such as prostitution, organized crime, and the legal profession. The team examined all the successful recruiting examples to determine any underlying principles or techniques that contributed to their effectiveness. They discovered these eight basic principles:

1. Challenging
2. Fast track
3. Convenience
4. Accessible
5. Selective
6. Recognition
7. Immediate Job
8. Cultural Group Network

The team then developed seven possible solutions for recruiting entry-level employees that included these basic principles. They subsequently selected two of these solutions and developed a plan to implement them.

TRIZ

A sophisticated application of the Honorable Thief method is known as TRIZ (pronounced "trees"). TRIZ is an acronym derived from a Russian language term that means "The Theory of Innovative Problem Solving."

In the 1940s, a Russian civil servant, Genrich Altshuller, was employed by the Soviet Navy to research patents. Altshuller's job was to find patents that had applications for the Soviet Navy. His team looked at 200,000 patents and he personally examined 40,000 patents. Ultimately, he found that all the ideas that resulted in patents could be described in forty "inventive principles." A few of these numbered forty inventive principles are:

1. Segmentation
10. Prior action

11. Cushion in advance
23. Feedback
28. Replacement of a mechanical system
35. Parameter change

Altshuller arrived at these forty principles by first identifying thirty-nine "parameters." When the parameters were compared to each other, technical contradictions resulted. Altshuller concluded that every innovative idea in 40,000 patents was a solution to one of these contradictions.

A few of the thirty-nine parameters are:

10. Force
11. Tension, pressure
14. Strength
16. Durability of non-moving object
18. Brightness
20. Harmful side effects

TRIZ is most often applied to solving engineering problems, particularly in the development of a new product. But TRIZ has also been applied to resolve business problems in sales, marketing, operations management, supply chain management, and human resources management. I will give a short description of an engineering application and then list a few principles applied to resolve business problems.

Consider a man's disposable razor. The blade should be sharp enough to cut the whiskers and yet dull enough so that it doesn't cut the skin. The blade must be sharp and dull at the same time! This is a technical contradiction between parameter 10, "Force," and parameter 30, "Harmful side effects." TRIZ suggests a way to create a man's razor blade that resolves this technical contradiction.

In our example of the razor blade, when I looked up the contradiction between parameters 10 and 30, I found that principles 1, 10, 11, 23, 28, and 35 have been applied to resolve this particular conflict in various disciplines for different products.

Design engineers used these six principles to stimulate their thinking when they invented a razor blade design. Several designs resolved the contradiction; the patent issued in 1901 to King Camp Gillette is for a double-blade arrangement with one sharp blade to cut the whiskers while the other blade is deliberately dull to push the skin away from the sharper blade. This is the application of principles 10 and 11.

Here are a few examples of the TRIZ principles applied to business problems:

1. *Segmentation.* A company that manufactured airplanes was responsible for maintaining their product after sales. The firm had skilled maintenance technicians to perform most of this responsibility but did not have individuals capable of providing full maintenance of the engine. The firm divided (segmented) the maintenance function into two parts: maintain aircraft engines and maintain "everything else." They were then able to outsource the maintenance of aircraft engines to another, better-equipped company. Segmentation permitted each aspect of the work to be performed in the best way possible.

10. *Prior Action.* Juvenal Courts in a city required social workers to file reports of their home visits before each hearing. The reports varied in format and often some necessary information was missing. The judges directed the social workers' agency to develop a single and complete report template to be completed by the social workers after each home visit. Prior action standardized formats of the reports and ensured the completeness of the information they contained.

11. *Cushion in advance and* 28. *Replacement of a mechanical system.* A company's customers complained that the company's products received were not always what the customers ordered. The company's quality department investigated and determined that the manual ordering process was flawed. The firm automated the ordering process, providing an online form that either agents of the company or customers could fill out, but including a confirmation dialog box. The dialog box gave individuals an opportunity to review each order before it is placed. The replacement of a mechanical system with an automated process and cushion in advance resulted in a significant reduction in customer complaints.

23. *Feedback and* 28. *Replacement of a mechanical system.* A project manager at a large company received financial data two weeks after employees performed work on the project and filed their time cards. When employees assigned to the project failed to perform the work that was scheduled, it was two weeks before the project manager could determine that the assigned task has not been performed. When it was discovered that this situation existed on all projects performed by this company, the company's management decided to automate the time keeping system and permit employees to enter their timekeeping information into the computer directly. The project manager was then able to learn when charges were made to her project in a day instead of two weeks. Many schedule issues were captured by project managers much earlier because the company implemented the replacement of a mechanical system with an automated process and cushion in advance.

TRIZ has been automated. Some software tools companies have significantly added to the database of 200,000 patents so it now reflects over a million patents from many countries. In addition, the software is friendly and easy to use. One can look up a technical contradiction and find a solution that someone else has discovered—in any discipline. There is a large contradiction table and some additional software that can be used to guide users through the matrix. Finding more information about TRIZ is as easy as using a good search engine on the Internet.

We will now conclude this subchapter by learning how the problem-solving team can apply the enhanced creative techniques to develop many solutions that eliminate the root causes and thereby permanently remove the main problem.

To begin Step Four, the problem-solving team decides on which of the creativity enhancement methods it wishes to apply. In my workshops I encourage the team to use Brute Think and Honorable Thief unless the solution is likely to involve hardware or software development, in which case I encourage them to use Brute Think and TRIZ.

Next, the problem-solving team needs to read the entire set of root causes aloud so that everyone in the team is reminded of what the team is trying to do—namely, find those actions that will eliminate all of the root causes. It is a good idea to have the root causes read aloud from time to time during the entire Step Four activity; the team cannot be reminded too often of their mission to remove those causes.

The team should then practice Brute Think or another creativity enhancing technique and make a list of several innovative solutions that could eliminate one or more of the root causes.

After applying the first of the creativity enhancement methods the team should try another one, such as Honorable Thief or TRIZ. Again, the team should read aloud the root causes to ensure all the members of the team are looking for ways to remove those causes and that candidate solutions to every one of the root causes are being listed.

When the creativity enhancement methods have been used, the team should try to create any additional candidate solutions in the context of the root causes. It is at this point that solutions that have been tried unsuccessfully in the past should be considered—it is possible the reason they didn't work in the past is that those old candidates needed to be combined with other, more innovative solutions.

What results from this step's activities is a list of potential solutions every one of which is an action which if taken may remove one or more of the root causes. This list of solutions is the input to Step Five—Select the Best Solution Set.

Summary of Actions Necessary in Step Four—Produce Many Solutions

1. Decide which group creativity enhancement methods to use. It is recommended two be selected.
2. At the beginning of the solutions generating activity and at frequent periods throughout the activity, the team should read the entire list of root causes aloud to ensure everyone is constantly focused on the objective of the activity—namely, to identify actions each of which will eliminate one more of the root causes, and that every one of the root causes have one or more candidate solutions identified to remove it.

3. The problem-solving team should then apply the first of the creativity enhancement methods to create a list of candidate solutions.

4. Next, the team should apply another creativity enhancement technique to create additional candidate solutions.

5. After the creativity enhancement methods have been used to produce a list of candidate solutions, the team should consider and add any mundane or less innovative solutions, including ones that have unsuccessfully been tried previously.

6. Finally, the team needs to collect all of the candidate solutions and prepare it to be examined for Step Five—Select the Best Solution Set.

Answer to the puzzle at the beginning of subchapter 4

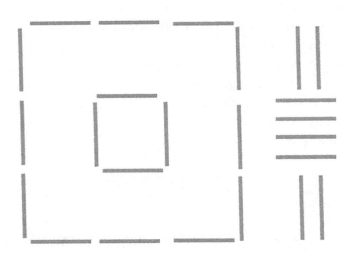

Step Five—Select the Best Solution Set

In this subchapter we will select those solutions that, taken together, will permanently solve the problem. We will first discover how to prioritize the candidate solutions and learn how each would resolve one or more of the root causes if it is implemented. We will put the solutions into a set that will become the basis of what we inform our management needs to be accomplished in order to implement a permanent solution to the main problem in Step Six.

There is no way that a simple solution can permanently solve a complex problem. In nearly all cases, the problem-solving team must look for a complex solution to its complex problems. The complete resolution of a complex problem will be a set of solutions which must all be implemented so that the entire set of root causes will be eliminated.

Selecting the best solution to the problem consists of six activities:

1. *Prioritize to identify the most promising solutions.*
2. *Consider the consequences of implementing each of the promising solutions.*
3. *Make a preliminary selection of the individual solution or solutions.*
4. *For the most likely solution or solutions, determine what other actions will have to be taken to make the selected solution fully effective.*
5. *Perform a cross-impact analysis to determine inter-dependencies of the entire solution set.*
6. *Package the solutions into a complete set for recommendation to management.*

Each of these will be examined in detail.

1. *Prioritize to identify the most promising solutions.*

I recommend using the same method for deciding which solution to try as we did to select which problem to address—the BCG Matrix or Silver Bullet Analysis.

The matrix considers the impact on the business against the ease of solving the problem. We are looking for solutions that are feasible to implement and have a high probability of permanently solving the problem.

The approach is to divide the list of all possible solutions into two categories, one half of the total number that are more likely to be effective than the other half. We mark the ones that are more effective with an *M* and the ones that are likely to be less effective with an *L*.

We then divide the list of all possible solutions into two different categories, one half of the total number that are more easily implemented given the resources and capabilities that we have than the other half, and half that are likely to be more difficult. We put an *E* next to those that are more easily implemented and those that are harder with an *H*. (For a more detailed illustration of this process, see the discussion of the BCG Matrix in Step One.)

We can then place the solutions into the quadrants of the matrix chart. Here is the matrix modified for selecting the most promising solutions:

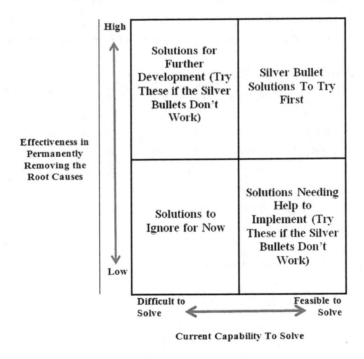

It is best to start with the solutions that fall into the "Silver Bullet" quadrant, but if other solutions are attractive, it might be possible to turn them into silver bullets by trading with a more effective solution and by making a solution easier by providing more resources, lowering the quality requirements, or by some other means.

2. *Consider the consequences of implementing each of the promising solutions.*

In order to determine which of the promising solutions to implement, we need to determine what impact implementation of each one would have. The problem-solving team obviously believes that the proposed solutions would remove one or more of the causes in the entire set of root causes that have been identified—it is this belief that prompted the team to identify the proposed solution in the first place. But the problem we are trying to solve is complex, so we must consider what impact any solution will have on the overall organization's processes and objectives. We do not want to implement a solution that inadvertently creates another problem in another process or area of the business, or one that turns out to be impractical because we do not have the necessary resources and capability to implement it.

The most basic methods for considering the impact of possible solutions are:

- *Project Planning*
- *Scenario Building*
- *Impact Assessment*

Project Planning

Project Planning is the activity within the project management process that identifies all of the tasks necessary to accomplish a project.

From the repertoire of project management tools, the three that are most useful in assisting problem-solving teams to determine what impact any proposed solution will have on the overall business processes are the Work Breakdown Structure, the Network Diagram, and the Responsibility Assignment Matrix. Together, these three tools show the team what the members need to know in order to assess the impact of a solution on other business processes.

Project management is the practice of breaking large business activities into practical ("do-able") tasks and ensuring those tasks are accomplished. I am describing here the more structured approach to project management, commonly referred to as stage-gated, phase-gated, or waterfall project management. While agile project management is deliberately less structured, the necessity to break large business activities (projects or programs) into do-able tasks is still essential. In solving complex

51

organizational problems, the structured approach that employs the three tools described in this subsection is recommended as more appropriate than agile project management.

For an example of these three tools applied to the activity of implementing a possible solution, consider an example where, in order to improve employee morale, we have decided we must reduce employee workload—with less pressure to work overtime and expend greater effort, the employees might increase their scores on the next employee satisfaction survey.

Work Breakdown Structure (WBS)

While it is not necessary to develop a detailed project plan for each proposed solution, the problem-solving team should develop a high-level breakdown of work so that at least all of the major categories of activities (human resources, scheduling, supply chain support, budgeting, etc.) are identified. The Work Breakdown Structure (WBS) is a graphic representation of the breakdown of the solution into its necessary elements. It can help the problem-solving team understand in a general way which tasks should be performed to implement the proposed solution.

Here is an example of a WBS for the proposed solution to reduce the workload by adding additional people to the normal work team:

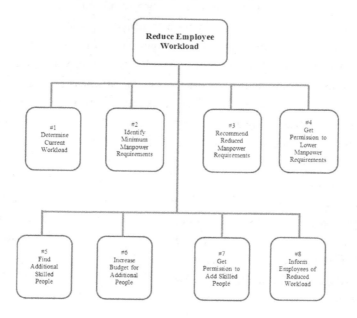

Network Diagram

The next tool we consider is the Network Diagram (sometimes incorrectly referred to as a "PERT chart"). This is a graphic representation of the relationships between the tasks that were identified in the WBS. The problem-solving team can use the Network Diagram to help understand the sequence in which the tasks must be performed. Without the awareness of this sequence, the problem-solving team cannot fully appreciate when the resources necessary to implement the proposed solution will be needed. While Gantt Charts are normally used to show the schedule of a project, for the problem-solving team's purposes, the Network Diagram is better, because by showing task relationships it gives better visibility into the resource loading necessary to implement the proposed solution. The Network Diagram for our workload reduction example would look like this:

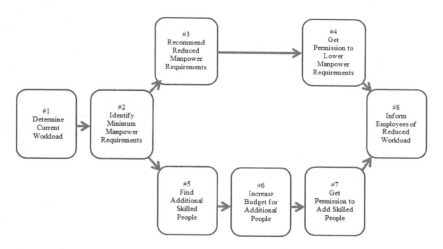

In the above example, note that there are two "paths": one for reducing the requirements and one for adding additional personnel.

Responsibility Assignment Matrix (RAM)

The third pertinent tool, the Responsibility Assignment Matrix (RAM), is often used by project teams to ensure every task has been assigned to someone and that every person who is assigned a task clearly understands it. The problem-solving team will need to know which people are available to implement the proposed solution and what their roles will be if the solution is adopted. The following example shows how a RAM for our manpower reduction example would look.

	Project Sponsor	HR/ Accounting	HR/ Placement	Team Leader	Team Member 2	Team Member 3
Considerations	Other activities but available by appointment	Available anytime	Appointment only but available	Full time	Half time, very competent	Full time, new employee
1. Determine current manpower usage		Support research		Accountable and do research		
2. Identify minimum manpower levels	Sign off	Support research	Support research	Accountable and do research		
3. Recommend minimum manpower level reductions		Support concept development			Accountable and develop concept	Support concept development
4. Get permission to lower manpower levels	Sign off			Support Team Member 2 during appeal	Accountable and negotiate with Sponsor	
5. Find additional people			Support research			Accountable and do research
6. Increase budget for additional people			Support research	Support research		Accountable and do research
7. Get permission to add skilled people	Sign off			Support Team Member 3 during appeal		Accountable and negotiate with Sponsor
8. Inform employees of reduced workload				Accountable		

Given the WBS, Network Diagram, and RAM, the problem-solving team can assess what would be involved is the proposed solution were adopted, and, accordingly, can determine if it is feasible.

Scenarios

The word "scenario" merely means "story." The problem-solving team may want to create a story about what will happen if each solution is implemented.

In this way, the expected benefits of, and the costs necessary to implement it, will become clear, so that the problem-solving team can rank the advantages of all of the proposed solutions. The problem-solving team may choose to develop a benefits-to-cost ratio for each proposed solution.

Here is a typical scenario for a proposed solution entitled Develop a Procurement Policy. This scenario ultimately describes a failure:

- We create a new, more comprehensive procurement procedure document;
- We publish and distribute the new document with guidance from upper management that it must be followed;
- The procurement department objects because they do not have enough people to perform the additional duties that the more comprehensive policy demands;
- The manager of the procurement department tries to implement the new policy at first but determines his staff is correct in pointing out that they do not have enough people to perform all the new duties;
- The manager of the procurement department and his staff prioritize the things they have to do and decide the new policy is not a high-enough priority to implement;
- The new policy is not followed.

Here is a checklist of questions to ask if you are developing a scenario of how a proposed solution might be implemented:

- Who will implement the changes?
- Who will be influenced by the changes?
- How will the affected people and processes react to the changes?
- What is likely to happen if the changes are not obviously beneficial to those people influenced by them?
- What is likely to happen if the changes are made and they do not fully solve the problem?

Impact Assessment

Once the tasks necessary to implement a solution have been identified, the impact that the proposed solution will have on each organizational function can be assessed (an Impact Assessment). Typical organizational functions include the following:

- Engineering
- Manufacturing
- Procurement
- Quality
- Safety
- Marketing
- Sales
- Supply Chain
- Program Management
- Business Operations
- Accounting
- Inventory Management

In smaller organizations or for simpler problems, the problem-solving team may be able to perform the Impact Assessment by itself, but for highly complex problems, it is suggested a special team with representatives of each functional division of the organization be convened to perform this activity. Most large companies have change control processes that have been institutionalized with a change control board (CCB), which includes representatives from each functional area of the organization. The CCB may perform the Impact Assessment efficiently for the problem-solving team.

Even in those cases where there is no CCB, the concept that drives organizations to implement control boards is relevant to the problem-solving process. It is important to identify which functional areas of the organization will be affected by the proposed solutions and determine if those changes are feasible.

3. *Perform a cross-impact analysis to determine inter-dependencies of the entire solution set.*

The problem-solving team must systematically develop and logically consider the influence that each of the proposed solutions may have on the other proposed solutions. This helps to ensure that the set of solutions that most effectively removes the root causes permanently is identified.

Cross-Impact Matrix

An example of this matrix is shown here, comparing alternate ways to implement a solution for aircraft cockpit windows:

	Solution 1. Replace Glass with Plastic	Solution 2. Replace Window with a Digital Panel	Solution 3. Create Heads Up Display (HUD) on Window	Solution 4. Train Pilots to Use Improved Display	Solution 5. Replace Pilots with Robotics
Solution 1. Replace Glass with Plastic					
Solution 2. Replace Window with a Digital Panel	*No impact— Mutually exclusive solutions*				
Solution 3. Create Heads Up Display (HUD) on Window	*No impact— HUD on plastic or glass is proven technology*	*Mutually Exclusive*			
Solution 4. Train Pilots to Use Improved Display	*No impact— HUD on plastic or glass is proven technology*	*Training pilots to use panel, easier than using HUD*	*Training pilots to use panel, easier than using HUD*		
Solution 5. Replace Pilots with Robotics	*No impact— Mutually exclusive solutions*	*No impact— Mutually exclusive*	*No impact— Mutually exclusive solutions*	*No impact— Mutually exclusive solutions*	

When the problem-solving team has forecast the implementation of each proposed solution and considered what impact each solution will have on both resolving the problem and on other business processes, the team is ready to select the best set of solutions for permanently removing the root causes.

4. *Make a preliminary selection of the one best solution.*

The problem-solving team is now ready to select that one solution that is most likely to solve the problem. This "best solution" should be feasible with a clearly visible means to be implemented, and it should obviously resolve most if not all of the root causes that have been identified.

5. *For the one best solution, determine what other actions will have to be taken to make the best solution fully effective.*

Complex, persistent problems that organizations experience never have a single, simple solution. The problem-solving team must identify which other activities must be performed in order to fully implement the solutions.

For example, if the best solution to the problem is to develop a new, more comprehensive policy, writing a new policy is essential. But it is not sufficient to permanently resolve the problem. If the new policy is not understood by everyone governed by it and if they are not held accountable for implementing it, it will probably not survive. Thus, if the problem-solving team's best solution is "to write a more comprehensive policy" the solution set must be:

1. Write a new policy document.
2. Train everyone affected to understand the new policy requirements.
3. Hold all affected people accountable for implementing the new policy.
4. *Package the solutions into a complete set for recommendation to management.*

The problem-solving team must include *all* of the solutions that have been determined are necessary to comprise a complete solution. The next step details exactly how to format the solution set for presentation to management.

Summary of Actions Necessary in Step Five—Select the Best Solution Set

1. Prioritize in order to identify the most promising solutions.
2. Consider the consequences of each of the promising solutions.
3. Make a preliminary selection of an individual solution or solutions.
4. For the most likely solution or solutions, determine what other actions will have to be taken to make the selected solution fully effective.
5. Perform a cross-impact analysis to determine inter-dependencies of the entire solution set.
6. Package the solutions into a complete set for recommendation to management as described in Step Six—Persuade Management to Implement the Solutions.

Step Six—Persuade Management to Implement the Solutions

In this subchapter we learn how to persuade management to implement the solutions. We begin with a discussion of methods for determining who the decision-makers are, how to influence them positively, and how to deal with the natural resistance they will have to making changes in the organization. We then develop a presentation and deliver it to management. The presentation includes a summary of what we have learned about the problem, its root causes, the best set of solutions, and our follow-up plan that will be described in more detail in Step Seven—Follow-Up, Ensuring the Problem Stays Solved.

If you are charged with solving business problems, you haven't done your job until the problems are actually solved. Recommending solutions isn't enough— you have to get the people who have the authority to make changes to agree to what you recommend. Solving problems includes selling your ideas to those who can make a difference.

Problem-solving teams must present the recommendations that they have developed in the first five steps of the problem-solving process to management. They must tell the managers what the managers should do differently to resolve the problems and they must tell them in a way that wins the approval of the managers. Often, technical people do not like to give presentations and some become especially upset when they have to "sell" their ideas. But good technical employees are those who actually solve business problems—selling their recommendations is a critical part of that job! The problem-solving team should spend time developing an effective presentation for their managers. They will benefit from advice and assistance given by those more adept at sales, so asking the sales department for help is strongly recommended. But the key to giving any presentation effectively is practice—the more the team practices the presentation, the greater the chances are that the managers will approve the recommendations.

Effective salespeople learn that to sell their product, service, or ideas, they have to first understand the *customer*. The best saleswomen and salesmen are not people who understand the product best—they are people who understand the customer best! The problem-solving team needs to understand the decision makers so that they can influence the decisions to incorporate the recommended solutions. There are three things the team must know in order to "sell" their ideas to upper management:

- *Who are the decision makers who need to approve the recommended solutions?*
- *What will positively influence the decision makers to approve the recommended solutions?*
- *What concerns do the decision makers have that would preclude their approval of the recommendations?*

These questions, reframed as actions to take, are as follows:

1. Learn Who the Decision Makers Are

The problem-solving team should discuss who in the organization has the power to direct the changes that will be necessary in order to implement the proposed solutions. It is important to identify the people who can authorize the solutions, not merely the immediate boss, and to present the solutions to them directly if possible.

If the problem-solving team does not normally have access to the actual decision-maker, it will be necessary for the team to present a case for implementing the solutions to appropriate senior managers in the organization who in turn can present the recommendations to the actual decision makers. The case presented to the intermediaries will have to be strong—it must not only convince them that the solutions are worth implementing, but also it must result in the managers' desire to advocate the case to the actual decision-makers. While it is always harder to work through someone else, it is sometimes necessary to do so.

2. Learn How to Win Their Approval

The decision to implement the proposed solution will be made by managers who are, like all people, motivated by factors that are not universally evident. What entices one person to make a decision may not influence another one to make the same decision. Good salespersons seek to understand the factors that motivate individuals to make decisions and they appeal to those individuals by stressing the factors that will be most effective. The problem-solving team should determine how the decision-makers make decisions.

People everywhere, including managers, take action when they believe it will be worthwhile to do so. All people are individually and personally motivated in how they take action and decide which course of action to take. The problem-solving team must develop a case for implementing their recommendations. Before the managers have a chance to ask, the problem-solving team should anticipate and answer the question "How will the managers benefit by approving and endorsing the recommendations?"

Psychological Tools

Psychological or style-based Instruments are tools that have been developed to help managers and salespeople determine how best to influence other people. Some powerful psychological tools that may be used in this fashion are these:

MBTI—Myers-Briggs Type Indicator
SDI—Strength Deployment Indicator
DiSC Profile—Dominance, Inducement, Submission, Compliance
LIFO—Life Orientation

Ordinarily, problem-solving teams do not have access to these instruments or their managers' scores, so other means have to be employed. The very best way to determine how a person processes information and makes decisions is to observe that person. If the problem-solving team discusses the behavior of their managers, they will be able to develop a fairly accurate understanding of what has motivated those managers in the past, and by appealing to them in the same fashion, the team can obtain the support of these managers to implement the changes necessary.

Of course, the problem-solving team must demonstrate that the costs for implementing the recommended solutions will be worth spending— that is, that the value derived from solving the problem will be more than what it will cost to make those changes. Managers nearly always are motivated to spend money only if they believe that doing so will save more money or gain greater profits in the future.

Generally speaking, managers are interested in profits, cash flow, and liquidity. The team should develop a business case for making the changes necessary to implement the recommended solutions. The business case may include the operating costs that will be saved, the increase in sales that will result, and the increase in revenue and cash flow that will result from solving the persistent problem. Managers also need to know how long any money they spend will be tied up before a profit is returned. The problem-solving team should calculate the payback point and honestly forecast when the managers will realize benefits if they invest in the proposed solutions.

If the continued existence of the problem places the organization or anyone in it in danger of legal action, most managers will be especially interested in reducing that danger. Many managers are concerned with the legality of their operations, and showing that a proposed solution will reduce the vulnerability to legal action will gain a lot of support in most organizations.

3. Anticipate Their Objections

There are three things I have learned that managers do not want to hear in a presentation. First, they do not want to hear that they, the managers, have not already been doing what should be done. Merely telling upper management all the things that they should have done but failed to do will not make them want to listen to what you have to say. During the team's presentation, showing the managers that the team is offering original, creative solutions *that could not already have been implemented by management* is more likely to win their approval. It is, therefore, important to stress the unique and innovative nature of the recommendations.

Second, managers do not want to be told that they are themselves completely responsible for the solution to the problem. Managers like to help employees achieve the employees' objectives, but they do not like to be told that they are themselves responsible for fixing what has gone wrong in the organization. The problem-solving team should identify the things that they are willing and able to do in order to achieve a lasting solution to the problem. They can then tell their managers, "We plan to do these things, but we cannot make all of the things happen that will be necessary to permanently resolve this problem—we need your help to accomplish those things we can't do ourselves." This approach has been shown to be far more effective in winning management support than merely stressing what actions the managers need to take.

Third, managers do not want to hear that the solution to the problem is going to be free. Managers know very well that nothing in business is free. Nothing! When the team says, "The new procedure will be written by people already assigned to the project, so there won't be any additional cost," savvy managers will instantly realize that the team has no idea of what it costs to run a business and what it costs to make changes to existing procedures and practices. The team must calculate the costs that will be required to perform any tasks necessary to implement the recommended solutions, including the costs of people working on these solutions when they would otherwise be working on something else. The term "opportunity costs" is used to describe costs of labor and resources that would otherwise be spent doing something else—the problem-solving team must calculate and present the opportunity costs, including any overtime or after-hours work anticipated. Management simply cannot believe any recommendation that professes to provide something for free.

Sales Pitch Agenda

The following presentation outline includes some important sales techniques.

Presentation Outline

A. **The Problem You Have Selected**
B. **Why Should Managers Listen to This Team?**
C. **Why Did You Select This Problem?**
D. **What Are the Root Causes of the Problem?**
E. **Which Set of Solutions Do You Believe Will Solve This Problem?**
F. **What Is Your Team Willing to Do Differently to Solve This Problem and Make Sure It Stays Solved?**
G. **What Must Management Do to Permanently Solve This Problem?**

H. What Is the Follow-Up Plan to Ensure Your Problem Stays Solved?

A. The Problem You Have Selected to Solve

The problem should be stated as the gap between the ideal situation and the current one. The team may start the presentation with something like this:

> How would you like to increase sales by 200 percent over the next two years? Our current sales are one million dollars each year but we think that, if we institute some better quality-control practices, we can increase sales to three million dollars per year. Today, we'd like to show you how.

> Or

> How would you like to cut operating costs by 40 percent without increasing risk or lowering the quality of the products we sell our customers? Last year the cost to manufacture our products was $210,500. We believe we can, by implementing simple and proven practices, reduce this to $126,300.

> Or

> How would you like to reduce the turnover in our technical staff? We are currently losing 250 technical people each year and we believe that, with some logical changes to our current staffing practices, we can reduce the number of people leaving us each year to fewer than 100!

Notice that in each of these examples, the problem has been redefined as the gap between the current and ideal situations, and that measureable numbers have been provided so the managers will be able to see progress if the recommendations are adopted.

B. Why Should Managers Listen to This Team?

Most presentations include introducing everyone on the team. Frankly, giving their names is not necessary (if the managers don't already know them, a brief listing of their names won't make managers remember them anyway). The reason you need to tell the managers who has contributed to the presentation is to develop credibility. Managers have a right to know that the people they are listening to have the ability to make effective assessments and deliver practical recommendations. Tell the audience the number of years of experience and the technical divisions represented by the team. It might sound like this:

> Our team has a total of fifty-six years of experience in our industry and we represent four divisions: Manufacturing, Engineering, Procurement, and Information Technology. We therefore represent a broad spectrum of the company's functions and have comprehensive experience in our business.

C. Why Did You Select This Problem?

There are two essential parts to this section of the presentation:

1. Show That It Is Important to the Company To Have This Problem Solved
2. Show Why You Believe This Problem Can Be Solved

Together, these two parts tell the managers why this problem was selected rather than some other one. If the problem to be solved was given to the problem-solving team, this section demonstrates that the problem team thoroughly understands why the problem is important.

The first part of this section deals with the value of solving the problem to the overall business operations. It should include hard numbers, if possible, and it should be convincing. Here are some examples:

> We performed a customer satisfaction survey and determined that last year we lost $250,000 in sales because 1.4 million customers felt that our competitor's product

was better than ours. We need to change the opinion of at least a million customers, and we know how to do that.

Or

We had the QA department compute the cost of rework and additional inspections that are necessary when we use suppliers that don't follow our vendor guidelines. We can easily improve our guidelines but we will show you today how, by restructuring our vendor selection processes, we can cut the cost of rework and additional inspections from $4.00 per item sold to less than $1.75.

The second part of this section answers the question "Can we solve this problem?" There are two ways to demonstrate that the problem can be solved. The best method is to show that someone, somewhere, in some organization, has solved this same problem or one nearly like it. If the problem is truly unique and nobody has solved it before, you may need to break the solution down into component tasks and use project management tools and practices to convince the managers you can solve it. But that method is not as good as showing that somebody else has already solved the problem. After all, if the solution has been achieved before, no one can claim that it can't be solved. The second part of this section might sound like this:

The sales department in PVC Industries, our biggest competitor, solved this problem last year. Their sales manager has joined our firm and he reports that in his old job they completely resolved this problem with the techniques we're about to show you today.

Or

The US Army has been faced with this problem for a long time, but at Fort Bliss they implemented some experimental practices that have, according to an article in the Harvard Business Review, improved their operation by 40 percent. We aren't the US Army and we don't have to answer to Congress or the Pentagon, so we think we can do even better than they did.

D. What Are the Root Causes of the Problem?

At this point it is necessary to show the managers what the problem-solving team feels causes the problem to exist. The report should not include the Fishbone Diagram and the rationale that the team used to arrive at the root causes, but needs only to state that the team has determine that the problem is caused by the entire set of root causes. It will sound like this:

> Our team has analyzed this problem and we feel that it has three causes. First, there are no written procedures, so the people working in that area all tend to follow different practices. Second, people in our company do not always follow the procedures even when they are written down. And finally, we do not believe there are any significant consequences for not following the written procedures.

E. Which Set of Solutions Do You Believe Will Solve This Problem?

Here you propose to the managers what solutions, when taken together, will permanently remove all of the root causes. A succinct description of the solution set is more likely to be clearly understood by managers and therefore more likely to be approved.

F. What Is Your Team Willing to Do Differently to Solve This Problem and Make Sure It Stays Solved?

Managers do not appreciate being told all the things that they, the managers, need to do. The problem-solving team will have much greater success if it demonstrates to the managers what the team members are willing to do to bring about a permanent solution to the problem. If there is research to do, the team should propose that members of the team stay involved by performing or assisting in performing the necessary research. If there are documents to be written, the team should propose that the members of the team write the documents, select and manage the writers, or assist in writing the documents. At the very least, the team should propose staying involved by following up to ensure the problem stays solved.

G. What Must Management Do to Permanently Solve This Problem?

This is really the heart of the presentation. The team has prepared and is making a sales pitch. It is essential that the team make clear what they believe managers must do for this problem to be permanently resolved.

What the team asks the managers to do must include the following:

1. Approve the recommendations.
2. Authorize all of the expenditures necessary (there are never, ever free solutions!).
3. Direct others to perform any tasks that the team cannot do to implement the solutions.
4. Authorize the team members to perform those activities that have been proposed.

H. What Is Your Follow-Up Plan to Ensure Your Problem Stays Solved?

In order for a solution to be permanently effective, it must be implemented at the beginning and forever after. The team should propose concrete, practical means for following up. The next subchapter describes some common means for determining that the problem has been permanently resolved. Since the solution isn't permanent until it has been implemented after the initial solution has been taken, the managers need to approve both the initial implementation of the recommended solutions and the follow-up as well.

Summary of Actions Necessary in Step Six—Persuade Management to Implement the Solutions

1. Determine who the managers are and how they make decisions.
2. Develop an effective presentation that includes a description of the problem and recommended actions that will permanently solve the problem. Effective sales methods should be incorporated into the presentation, and the problem-solving team should volunteer to assist in implementing the solutions and to conduct follow-up activities necessary to ensure the problem stays solved.
3. Make the presentation to management. If they approve the recommendations, then begin the implementation and plan to follow-up as described in Step Seven.

Step Seven—Follow-Up—Ensure the Problem Stays Solved

In this subchapter we will learn two methods to thoroughly follow-up the problem-solving process to make sure the problem stays solved.

Persistent problems can be permanently solved, but to solve them requires more than merely developing recommendations. The recommendations must be implemented and then the recommended actions that constitute the solution must be followed up.

Follow-up Activities

There are two ways that the problem-solving team can follow up to ensure that the problem has been and has stayed solved.

The first method is to institute formal scanning for the metrics that were identified in the definition phase of the problem-solving process. If the team has followed the process described in this book, they identified ways to measure improvement when they defined the problem as the gap between the ideal and current situations. Then, in selling their solution, they promised their managers that those metrics would be used to demonstrate that the problem was permanently solved once the solutions were fully implemented. Accordingly, when recommending a solution to management, the problem-solving team should propose, as an integral and essential part of the solution set, a means to scan for those metrics after the primary solutions have been implemented. The following table gives some examples of the metrics that might be employed to demonstrate first that the problem has been solved and secondly that it has stayed solved over time:

Examples	
Metric	**Indicator**
Employee Morale	Scores on annual employee satisfaction surveys
Customer Satisfaction	Customer Complaints, Customer Satisfaction Surveys
Sales	Market Share, Sales Statistics
Product Performance	Warranty Claims, Defects, Re-Works

Overhead Costs	Facilities and Tools Expenses
Product Price	Costs of Manufacturing, Delivery Costs, Margin

If the metrics collected after the solutions have been implemented show that the desired results have been achieved, the problem-solving team should inform management and find another persistent problem to solve.

Abbreviated Problem Solving Process

Sometimes the metrics do not demonstrate that the problem has been solved, in which case the second approach to follow-up should be employed. In this approach, the problem-solving team should follow an abbreviated version of the problem-solving process to determine what went wrong and what can be done to permanently solve the problem.

1. *Re-assess the importance to the organization of solving the problem.* The value for the organization to have this problem solved may have changed or perhaps it wasn't fully understood to begin with.
2. *Analyze the problem again.* This may surface other factors that contributed to the root causes but which were overlooked or considered less important than they actually are.
3. *Scan to see if any new developments have emerged that would influence the assessment of the problem and the creation of solutions to permanently remove the root causes.* This may surface new information that the team can use to improve its assessment and solution creation.
4. *Generate new solutions based on the modified assessment if necessary.*
5. *Re-examine the metrics and produce new ones or modify the ones for which the team is scanning.*
6. *Present to management the recommendation for changes in analysis, solutions, and metrics.* It is important to gain the support of management in making any changes necessary to permanently solve the problem.

Summary of Actions Necessary in Step Seven—Follow-Up, Ensuring the Problem Stays Solved

1. Identify how to measure the state of the solution. These should be the same metrics that were used to assess the problem and find solutions to it.
2. If the metrics fail to demonstrate the problem has been solved, perform an abbreviated version of the problem-solving method to identify what when wrong and implement corrections.

4. Create a Problem-Solving Culture

For over four decades I have led problem-solving teams in the practice of the problem-solving process described in this book. Most of the teams have been successful in identifying problems and permanently resolving them. But some have not. I was curious to discover why some organizations are successful and some are not. What is it about one company that makes solving problems possible while others seem to find it too difficult to accomplish? What do some firms do that makes them better able to find and apply effective measures to resolve recurring issues more consistently than their competitors? Based on my observations I have come to believe that there are certain characteristics that are evident in those organizations that permanently solve persistent problems more effectively.

In this chapter I Identify ten of those features that I believe define the culture of an organization capable of permanently solving persistent problems. These characteristics are *developed* in successful organizations (they can be learned). My hope is that you will influence your organization to adopt these characteristics in the expectation that if you do, your organization will be better positioned to detect and permanently solve many of the persistent problems that plague industry today.

I believe these characteristics are common to every effective problem-solving culture:

1. *It is intolerant of unsolved problems.*
2. *It is firmly convinced that problems can be solved.*
2. *It is realistic in its self-assessment.*
3. *It possesses a process for immediately detecting and responding to problems.*

4. *It possesses a process to manage problem solving in a logical, systematic way.*
5. *It deliberately develops problem-solving skills of all managers and employees.*
6. *It is fact-based.*
7. *It holds people accountable for solving problems.*
8. *It is creative in finding and implementing solutions.*
9. *It is results-oriented.*

1. It is intolerant of unsolved problems

All organizations have individuals who complain, but in many organizations the fault-finding seldom results in action aimed at solving actual issues. In a problem-solving culture, however, there is a general feeling that dissatisfaction should become the focus of pro-active efforts to find and fix what's wrong. Everyone from the CEO to the janitor are uncomfortable with unsolved problems. They are firmly convinced that the organization would be a better place to work if the problems they encounter were solved. They do not merely complain about problems in the workplace and in the marketplace—they expect to solve them.

The key to developing this intolerance for unsolved problems is to nurture the dissatisfaction. Senior managers and supervisors at all levels can nurture dissatisfaction by pointing out the impact unsolved problems have on the individuals in the workplace. Organizational problems affect everyone, and by reminding everyone what the personal cost of an unsolved problem to every individual, the individuals at all levels will be more willing to find solutions than if they believe a solution will make managers richer but will not change their own environment in a positive way.

2. It Believes That Problems Can Be Solved

No one denies that some problems cannot be solved. But all or most of the individuals in a problem-solving culture believe that it is possible to solve most of them and they especially believe that the important problems which affect the organization's ability to reach its business goals can always be reframed in a fashion that will permit them to be resolved.

The only way I know to develop firm beliefs that problems can be solved is to solve a lot of them. If people see something happen they can't deny it is possible to happen. This is true of problem solving. When difficult, complex, and recurring problems are solved, the problem-solving culture publicizes that success, building confidence that persistent problems can be solved in this organization.

3. It Is Realistic in Its Self-Assessment

A problem-solving culture recognizes that many problems are beyond the organization's current capability to resolve and, accordingly, it prioritizes and focuses on addressing the problems that it can solve now. Only those problems that the organization has sufficient resources and competency to solve at this time should be undertaken now. A successful problem-solving culture is honest in determining what it can and what it cannot do at this time.

The best way to develop a culture that is realistic in its self-assessment is to apply the process that is described in this book. Repeating Step One will ensure the resources of the organization will not be squandered trying to solve problems that cannot be solved now and success in solving persistent problems will nurture a culture that is honest in its assessment of its capabilities.

4. It Possesses a Process for Immediately Detecting and Responding to Problems

Not all problems are persistent ones like those described in this book. Occasionally sudden and surprising problems arise. Some organizations, those with an effective problem-solving culture, are constantly on the lookout for unexpected problems and are prepared to respond immediately when they do arise. If surprising problems are not dealt with immediately, they will either cause severe damage to the organization or they will become persistent problems. It is essential, therefore, that organizations scan for unexpected problems and solve them as soon as possible.

The process described in this book for solving persistent problems can be modified to provide solutions to the sudden and surprising ones, but that is ordinarily not necessary. Sudden problems usually have obvious causes or ones that can be discovered fairly simply. By examining the environment in which the problem arose and asking what has changed, we are able to discern the cause of most sudden problems. In the event the causes of these sudden problems are not readily evident, more thorough assessments can be made similar to those described in Step Two.

To develop a culture that possesses a process for immediately detecting and responding to problems, the organization needs to institute the process and encourage everyone to follow it.

5. It Possesses a Process to Manage Problem Solving in a Logical, Systematic Way

Problem-solving cultures have processes in place that manage the problem-solving activities and ensure those activities are aimed at goals in line with the organization's business objectives. The process described in this book should be an integral part of the general problem-solving management system. An additional process for scanning the business environment and internal business condition to determine if sudden problems emerge that would otherwise go undetected should be included. This problem-solving management system should also ensure that all necessary training is conducted effectively.

The organization needs to institute the process, and encourage managers to implement it, in order to develop a culture that possesses a process for managing problem solving in a logical, systematic way,.

6. It Deliberately Develops Problem Solving Skills of All Managers and Employees

Problem-solving cultures conduct training or coaching programs that deliberately develop the problem-solving skills necessary. This training and coaching should not be limited to a handful of individuals who are assigned to problem-solving teams—it should be provided to everyone at all levels of the organization. Of course the training program should be carefully designed to ensure that each individual in the organization develops the capability to solve problems that are important to their own project, department, or managerial level. Providing training to individuals who cannot immediately apply what they learn is ineffective and wasteful training. Accordingly the training and coaching should be provided to those individual who need it when they need it and in the fashion that develops the skills effectively. This training should include developing skill in justifying ideas, decisions, proposals, and suggestions with evidence (see Characteristic 7).

To develop a culture that deliberately develops problem-solving skills of all managers and employees, the organization needs to identify the skills necessary at each level and in each area, and then provide appropriate training or coaching.

7. It Is Fact-Based

Everyone in a problem-solving culture constantly ask for evidence. Managers and supervisors, technical staff, and support functions all demand that ideas be supported by facts. Intuitive ideas are wonderful and are strongly encouraged in finding innovative solutions to problems, but the constant concern of everyone in a problem-solving culture is, "What is the evidence?" Any idea, any information received in a problem-solving culture stimulates the question, "Do you have any evidence for that?" There still is a place for intuition; facts and figures do not replace human intuition. But intuition without evidence is not sound business practice, either. Problem-solving cultures nurture managers and employees who demand facts to support any suppositions they encounter.

The best way to developing a culture that is fact-based is to demand evidence based on facts and figures in all business meetings, and to train individuals to provide justification for their ideas, decisions, proposals, and suggestions with evidence (see Characteristic 6).

8. It Holds People Accountable for Solving Problems

Problem-solving cultures hold individual accountable for solving problems.
Accountability demands four things:

a. *Clear expectations*
b. *Necessary resources*
c. *Metrics*
d. *Real consequences*

a. Clear Expectations

It is unfair to hold people accountable if they do not clearly understand what they are expected to do. It is also unreasonable. Top-level managers should make it evident that the organization is dedicated to finding and resolving those problems that the organization can solve. This guidance needs to be explicit— what exactly do the managers expect people to do? Another way to clarify expectations about problem solving is to train the employees in the problem-solving methods that are described in this book.

b. Necessary Resources

It is unfair to hold people accountable if they do not have the resources to accomplish what is expected of them. Management in a problem-solving culture must ensure that the employees have all the tools and support necessary to identify and solve problems, including any necessary training.

c. Metrics

It is unfair to hold people accountable if they cannot measure their own progress in the same way their progress is being judged by their superiors. Managers in problem-solving cultures must identify and make clear the metrics that the managers use to evaluate the performance of the employees.

d. Real Consequences

Most organizations do not enforce real consequences—positive or negative—in regard to performance expectations for employees or groups. When milestones are not met, when schedules are missed, when the quality of the services and products delivered fall short of expectations, nothing happens in many organizations. We often think we have real consequences for poor performance, and maybe over time we do—given enough mistakes, an employee might actually be fired. But the truth is that most of the time in most organizations poor performance is not punished and good behavior is not rewarded. Do a good job and your bosses will dump more work on you! In effective problem-solving cultures, however, people are held accountable for identifying and solving problems. When the problems are identified and solved the individuals who participated are rewarded, and when the problems go unnoticed or unresolved, the people who should notice and fix them are actually called upon to explain their actions or to be corrected or disciplined in some way.

Thus, in order to develop a culture that holds people accountable for solving problems, it will be necessary for the organization to implement and enforce policies and practices to provide clear expectations, provide the necessary resources, institute metrics so individuals can see for themselves how they are doing, and finally ensure real consequences result from each individual's actions.

9. It Is Creative in Finding and Implementing Solutions

A problem-solving culture is creative. The factors that ensure that the individuals and teams in a problem-solving culture are creative include the following:

a. *Understand the creative thought process.*
b. *Provide opportunities for creativity to flourish.*
c. *Reward success.*
d. *Removed fear.*

a. Understand the Creative Thought Process

Everyone in a problem-solving culture understands the human creative process:

Divergent and convergent thinking.

b. Provide Opportunities for Creativity to Flourish

In problem-solving cultures, group creativity and individual innovation are given time to develop and flourish. Employees are given time away from their normal jobs to think in unique and different ways. Workshops and training programs are provided in which the employees can discuss innovative ways to identify what's wrong in the organization and what can be done to improve products and processes. Techniques and practices to enhance creativity similar to those described in this book are implemented throughout the organization.

c. Reward Success

In an effective problem-solving culture, successes in applying creativity to persistent issues and finding innovative solutions are enthusiastically and publically celebrated.

d. Remove Fear

Paradoxically, many companies actually celebrate failures—if they aren't devastating—in order to encourage staff members to experiment or perhaps take reasonable risks where a successful outcome is not certain. An effective problem-solving organization makes a concerted effort to uncover fear of trying things out and neutralizes those fears to the degree possible.

In order to nurture a culture that is creative in finding and implementing solutions to problems, the organization must help everyone understand the creative process, provide opportunities for creativity to flourish, reward successes, and removed fear.

10. It Is Results-Oriented

Nothing is more important to the problem-solving culture than getting results. The truly effective problem-solving culture considers identifying and resolving persistent problems integral to everything it does, and celebrates successes when those are achieved.

The key to developing a culture that results-oriented is to celebrate successes when those are achieved and to encourage everyone to strive for the desired result when they experience setbacks or otherwise fall short of fully achieving the stated results.

5. Some Examples—Case Studies

In this chapter I have provided examples of how six organizations have succeeded in finding permanent solutions to persistent problems by applying the process describe in this book. Each of these cases represents a client organization that I personally guided through the process. All six of these organizations used the following ten tools:

- Brainstorming
- Whining Session
- BCG (Silver Bullet) Matrix
- Gap Definition
- Root Causes Analysis
- Ishikawa Diagram
- Brute Think
- Honorable Thief
- Scenarios
- Sales Pitch Agenda

In those cases where additional tools were used, I have indicated that.

Case Study 1: Brainpower Drain

Stated Problem

A large utilities company was unable to replace all of the people who were leaving to retire, to go to another utility firm, or to leave the utilities business. The firm had lost, and expected to continue to lose, its most skillful workers over the next five years and there was little hope of replacing them fast enough to continue operations at the current rate.

Tools Used

This organization used the ten tools cited at the beginning of this chapter. They also used third-party audits and benchmarking to establish the ideal situation in redefining the problem, and the used the three project management tools Work Breakdown Schedule, Network Diagram, and Responsibility Matrix to plan the implementation of the solutions.

Redefined Problem

The current work load required 675 skilled workers in a certain category. The firm had 600 skilled people in that category. In each of the next five years the firm expected to lose 75 people. To staff fully to fill the required work responsibilities, the firm would have to hire and/or train 450 people to bring the skilled worker total to 675.

Root Causes

Most of the skilled people leaving were retiring. However, there are not enough people in the workforce who wanted to and were capable of being trained to become skilled workers at the rate of 75 people per year. While the company had excellent training programs, it could not bring the people that were currently being hired up to this level fast enough. The job requirements were higher than the available recruits could acquire at that rate.

Solution Set

- The jobs requiring the skilled personnel were restructured to eliminate the need for the high level of competency that had been required before. Of the 450 open jobs, 250 were replaced with jobs requiring less qualified people. This reduction in requirements was achieved primarily through automating as many of the required activities as possible;

- Retiring people were hired back as contract labor or as consultants to train the 200 personnel who needed to be at the higher competency level. The re-hired retirees were not asked to continue the work that they had been doing previously, since that would simply prolong the inevitable departure of the most skilled workers until they could no longer function;
- As much of the work as possible was outsourced. However, the companies to which the work was outsourced struggled to obtain the high caliber of worker that the utility company required, so the total number of highly skilled jobs that could be filled by suppliers was limited. This did serve as a temporary stop-gap measure, however, and bought time to implement other solutions.

Results

The utility company was able to convince the public utilities commission that they had the situation under control, and the firm remained profitable.

Case Study 2: Practices of Two Merged Companies

Stated Problem

A large chemical company purchased another company. The two merged companies comprised one of the world's largest firms. The purchasing company and the acquired firm had different practices, including different ways to perform certain research projects. The researchers from the acquired firm felt they were being forced to adopt practices that were less effective than the ones they had successfully practiced for years, but the purchasing company's researchers felt that their heritage practices were superior to the practices of the newly acquired firm. Morale in the laboratories was poor, and there was often a lack of collaboration. It was felt the effectiveness of the research was severely degraded.

Tools Used

This organization used the ten tools cited at the beginning of this chapter. They also used Third-Party Audits and the three project management tools

Work Breakdown Schedule, Network Diagram, and Responsibility Matrix to plan the implementation of the solutions.

Redefined Problem

Twice each year, a third-party audited all of the major research projects being performed in this company. Each research project was scored for overall research effectiveness on a scale from 1 (poor) to 10. The average score in the purchasing company prior to the merger was 8.73, but after the merger the average score (for the entire organization) was 5.39. The problem was redefined as follows: We need to raise the average research project effectiveness rating of 5.39 to 9.0 or better. (It was felt that a perfect score of 10 was an unrealistic goal).

Root Causes

One cause of this problem was that researchers in each company were practicing different research procedures so there was a breakdown in cooperation and communication. When researcher in each company practiced the procedures that were prescribed by their own heritage company before the merger, those procedures were effective. But differences between the two procedures caused the breakdown in collaboration after the merger. In addition, many researchers failed to follow the research protocols requested by their own heritage firm. These researchers became involved with the subject of their specific research and forgot to consider and implement company-directed practices.

Solution Set

The solution proposed by the problem-solving team included forming a committee with researchers from both companies to review and agree upon a single written procedure. Their solution also included establishing a "training and awareness" campaign to ensure that all leaders of research projects were aware of the advantages of following the prescribed protocols and everyone understood what they were supposed to do under those revised procedures. The third-party audit teams were instructed to check to see that the company-wide procedures were being followed. To gain visibility into whether the solutions were working, the team proposed accelerating the third-party audits to quarterly for one year.

Results

Average scores from the third-party audits improved, moving to 8.71 from 5.39 in one year. In a follow-up activity, some of the researchers who had been with the purchased company reported feeling "a lot better" about how they were now being incorporated into the merged company's operations.

Case Study 3: Management Decisions Take Too Long

Stated Problem

Large projects at a major aerospace firm were often late in delivering the scheduled project results. The project managers reported that the main reason for the lateness was because they invariably had to wait for management decisions such as authorization to spend resources, directives to assign personnel, and approval to proceed to the next phase of the projects.

Tools Used

This organization used the ten tools cited at the beginning of this chapter. They also used the Waste ("Muda") checklist to identify problems, and the three project management tools Work Breakdown Schedule, Network Diagram, and Responsibility Matrix to plan the implementation of the solutions.

Redefined Problem

The planned due dates for project deliverables for twenty-six large projects were compared with actual delivery dates. The on-time delivery rate was only 59 percent. The measured projects involved a total of 159 separate deliverables. One deliverable had been ninety-two days late, five were from sixty to ninety days late, twelve were from thirty to fifty-nine days late, twenty-two were from fifteen to twenty-nine days late, and twenty-six were from one to fourteen days late! The problem was redefined as follows:

Add forty-one points to the average on-time delivery percentage so that deliverables are completed on schedule 100 percent of the time.

Root Causes

Upon careful examination, it was found that waiting for management decisions was indeed the bottleneck in most cases, but there were other reasons for late delivery. Some project team members were inexperienced and didn't understand project management practices. The managers' timing was thought to result from managers not understanding the impact that their late decisions had on the projects and the lack of accountability for making timely decisions. While project managers were criticized for missed deliveries, the managers were not held responsible for how their decision practices contributed to the schedule delays.

Solution Set

The problem-solving team recommended that the project management office assign coaches to bring the project management skills of the project team members up to speed. They also suggested that the project management practices be modified to include a formal session with managers who had decision authority to ensure those managers were fully aware of the impact that late decisions would have on the project's planned schedule. And finally, the problem-solving team suggested that when a manager's late decision caused a late delivery, this information would be brought to the attention of the offending manager's immediate manager.

Results

Project plans and actual deliveries were re-examined in six months and the on-time delivery rate of 59 percent improved to 93 percent. The head of the project management office felt that the recommended solutions, if continued, would result in very nearly 100 percent on-time delivery performance.

Case Study 4: Quality Fade

Stated Problem

A US medical products company had contracts for components to be supplied by three Chinese manufacturing firms. The manufacturing standard was "build-to-print," that is, each manufacturer followed design specifications provided by the US company. The arrangement with each supplier was the result of extensive negotiation and collaboration between the US company's representatives and the managers of the Chinese firms. Quality standards were stressed and the manufacturing firms had all agreed to abide by the US company's design without any modifications. After a few months, however, one of the Chinese companies decided to make "improvements" to the design and reduced the amount of a precious metal used at a connection point that interfaced with other components. The result was that this firm's components did not meet the US company's design specification and the medical product system often failed final testing.

Tools Used

This organization used the ten tools cited at the beginning of this chapter. They also used Voice of the Customer, Failure Modes and Effects Analysis, and the Project Risk Matrix to identify problems, and they used the cross-impact matrix to help understand how candidate solutions could be combined into a single, effective set of solutions.

Redefined Problem

The problem was redefined: Bring the noncomplying manufacturing firm's compliance rate to 100 percent compliance with the US company's design specification.

Root Causes

In industries such as this one, when any supplier takes it upon itself to modify the design of a service or product without complete change control procedures it is termed "quality fade." The obvious problem appeared to be that one supplier was guilty of quality fade, but that did not fully explain why this had happened. In addition, the occurrence of this problem with one supplier raised the prospect that it might reappear with other suppliers at other times. After examining the situation, the problem-solving team determined that a supplier (in any country) makes those deviations from the agreed-to specifications to improve its own advantage. Accordingly, the root cause of this problem was that one of their suppliers didn't recognize the value to itself of fully subscribing to its customer's design. The team recognized that while the US company had made its design requirements clear at the beginning, it had not re-enforced those specifications over time, and one supplier had lost sight of any need to meet the requirements.

Solution Set

The problem-solving team proposed that three changes be made by its own company. First, they said, their company's project plans should include a significant amount of money and time to conduct frequent discussions with the suppliers to ensure they continue to understand the design requirements. Second, the team developed a presentation to be given to all suppliers that "educated" the supplier management on the doctrine that meeting customer requirements is the best way to ensure long term growth and profitability. And third, the company was to devote time and effort to work with the three Chinese firms to better understand those firms' business operations and help them develop strategic opportunities.

Results

Upon implementation of the solution, all three Chinese firms supplied 100 percent compliant components.

Case Study 5: Building Trust

Stated Problem

An international pharmaceutical firm was testing a potential new product in simultaneous clinical trials in Europe, Canada, and India. The trial teams each included members located in different countries who had to interact with each other to perform the trial of the new drug. The clinical trial teams had all been rapidly assembled and the members of the trial teams did not all know their other team members well. There had not been time for the team to develop interpersonal trust—an essential ingredient in performing a successful clinical trial.

Tools Used

This organization used the ten tools cited at the beginning of this chapter. They also used some psychological tools to understand how team members think, process information, and make decisions.

Redefined Problem

Team members complained a lot and the scheduled tasks often took longer than were normally experienced in other clinical trials where teams had more time to develop trust. Surveys were conducted and 35 percent of the clinical trial team members reported they didn't trust the other members of their teams to do what was needed. A list of required deliverables was created and actual delivery dates were compared with actual delivery dates for the same items produced on previous projects. Some 45 percent of the items compared were later than had been experienced on previous projects. The problem-solving team redefined the problem as follows: From the 35 percent of the non-trusting trial team members, obtain updated responses from all of them that they trust other team members. Also, as to the required items that had been delivered late, improve the on-time delivery rate to that experienced on previous trials.

Root Causes

The problem-solving team determined that the clinical trial team members did not trust each other because they had not worked together long enough to observe reliable (trustworthy) behavior from each other. The urgency of business situations also precluded developing trust among team members. The problem-solving team determined that the trial team members were reluctant or unable to share personal information about themselves and so all the attempts that the company had made to build stronger, more trusting teams had failed. They described the root cause of the problem as failure of the trial teams to fully engage in the team building exercises, failure of the team building program facilitators to incorporate cultural differences into their exercises, and failure of the trial team to accept responsibility for meeting schedules even if other members failed to perform their responsibilities on time.

Solution Set

The problem-solving team recommended that the entire team-building program be revised by experts in international teams to incorporate diverse cultural issues. Next, they suggested that the trial team members be given more detailed and more effective directions by their managers, including a thorough explanation of the importance of each deliverable. Another recommendation was that managers request a commitment from each trial team member to meet his or her delivery schedules regardless of anyone else's behavior. And finally, the project schedules were to be published and widely distributed so that everyone knew who was responsible for specific activities, and if some deliverable was tardy, who was responsible for its slippage.

Results

The team-building program was completely revamped and all participants who were interviewed afterward reported they found it far more enjoyable, relevant, and effective. A special "executive briefing" was designed and presented to managers who would assign individuals to serve on trial teams, and it included emphasis on achieving a personal commitment to perform regardless of what other team members did. It also made clear the benefits of having all of the deliverables produced on time. Finally, the project management office reported that 95 percent of the deliverables were delivered on time, an improvement of fifty percentage points!

Case Study 6: A Dysfunctional Team

Stated Problem

The senior managers of a small but successful computer display hardware systems firm in the Silicon Valley felt that their executive team was dysfunctional. Nearly all of the executive team members felt that one member, the vice president of procurement, was to blame for the dysfunction. This VP was nearly always in disagreement with the other executives, including the CEO, and team meetings were typically tedious sessions full of arguments and very little agreement. The executive team meetings degenerated into arguments, and then the CEO usually made his decisions, apparently independently of the other executives' positions. Morale of the executives was low and that seemed to translate into poor morale at the other levels of the organization. In surveys by an independent consultant, employees in Procurement felt they were all at odds with everyone else in the firm, and employees in other divisions felt that Procurement was inhibiting growth of the entire firm.

Tools Used

This organization used the ten tools cited at the beginning of this chapter. They also used the cross-impact matrix to explore the interrelations between candidate solutions and some psychological tools to understand how team members think, process information, and make decisions.

Redefined Problem

The executives, when independently polled, said they felt their weekly meetings should normally take two hours but those meetings averaged six hours. On surveys, 60 percent of the employees rated their satisfaction at between 1 and 3 (on a scale of 1 to 5) and only 40 percent rated themselves as satisfied working at this firm. The problem-solving team redefined the problem as follows: reduce the executive team meeting duration to two hours from six hours, and increase the percentage of employees that rank themselves as satisfied to 90 percent from 40 percent.

Root Causes

The problem team felt that there were three causes of the problem. First, because the CEO made his decisions independently of the executive team's meeting, there was no incentive for the executive team to reach consensus. Second, the executives could not confront the VP of Procurement: they argued issues with him but were unable or unwilling to tell him that they felt he was a detriment to the firm's operations. Finally, it was unclear to what extent the disagreement among executives contributed to the low employee morale. Since the executives were upset about their intra-team contention, they were blindly attributing general low employee morale to that factor when, in fact, other issues may have been present.

Solution Set

First, regarding decisions that could be made by the executive team, the CEO was asked to poll the executives and abide by the decision of the majority on those issues. This placed greater responsibility on the executive team to reach consensus in their interactions. Second, the executive team members were given some basic training by an outside consultant in how to disagree without generating unproductive debate. Third, each executive was challenged to determine why his or her division's employee satisfaction scores were low and to take appropriate action to have the employees raise them. The firm instituted a competition between the divisions to see who could make the greatest improvement.

Results

The CEO changed his decision-making style and proceeded to base most of his decisions on the consensus opinion of the executives. The VP of Procurement was confronted not merely by the CEO but also by every other executive and he decided he would be better off working somewhere else. One of the other executives assisted him in locating a job he considered an improvement and he was replaced with a person who was more compatible with the rest of the executive team. Finally, a major program to raise employee satisfaction was initiated and the surveys showed significant improvement. It is not known how much the executive dissension contributed to the low employee satisfaction, but since many other issues were raised, it is clear that it was not the sole root cause of low employee satisfaction scores.

Index of Problem Solving Tools

Step One—Prioritize and Select a Problem

BCG (Silver Bullet) Matrix

Step Two—Redefine the Problem

Gap Definition

Step Three—Find the Root Causes

Root Cause Analysis

Ishikawa ("Fishbone") Diagram

Multi-Voting

Step Four—Produce Many Solutions

Brute Think

The Honorable Thief

TRIZ

Step Five—Select the Best Solution Set

Project Planning

Work Breakdown Structure (WBS)

Network Diagram

Step Six—Persuade Management to Implement the Solutions

Step Seven—Follow-Up—Insure the Problem Stays Solves

Recommended Additional Reading

Adair, John. *Decision Making and Problem-Solving Strategies: Learn Key Problem Solving Strategies; Sharpen Your Creative Thinking Skills; Make Effective Decisions, 2010.*

Anderson, Bjørn, and Tom Fagerhaug. *Root Cause Analysis: Simplified Tools and Techniques*, 2nd Ed., 2006

Bradley, Simon, *Critical Thinking: Proven Strategies To Improve Decision Making Skills, Increase Intuition And Think Smarter*, 2016

Brassard, Michael, *The Problem Solving Memory Jogger 2nd Ed.*, 2011

De Bono, Edward. *Lateral Thinking: A Textbook of Creativity* 2009. Originally published in 1970. ———. *Six Thinking Hats*, 1999.

Kahneman, Daniel, *Thinking, Fast and Slow*, 2013

Kallet, Michael, *Think Smarter: Critical Thinking to Improve Problem-Solving and Decision-Making Skills*, 2014

Kendrick, Tom. *Identifying and Managing Project Risk: Essential Tools for Failure-Proofing Your Project*, 2009

Nadler, Gerald, and Shozo Hibino. *Breakthrough Thinking: The Seven Principles of Creative Problem Solving*, 2nd ed., 1998.

Okes, Duke. *Root Cause Analysis: The Core of Problem Solving and Corrective Action*, 2009.

Ratzesberger, Oliver and Sawhney, Mohanbir, *The Sentient Enterprise: The Evolution of Business Decision Making*, 2017

Rubinstein, Moshe, and Iris Firstenberg. *Patterns of Problem Solving*, 2nd ed., 1994.

Russell, Mike, *Wrong Until Right, How to Succeed Despite Relentless Change*, 2015

Setili, Amanda, Fearless Growth: *The New Rules to Stay Competitive, Foster Innovation, and Dominate Your Markets*, 2017

Singhal, Jai, *Solving Problems: The Agile Way*, 2014

Sutherland, Jeff, and Sutherland, JJ, *SCRUM: The Art of Doing Twice the Work in Half the Time*, 2014

Thaler, Richard H,. *Misbehaving: The Making of Behavioral Economics*, 2016

Wilson, Jennifer, *Critical Thinking: A Beginner's Guide to Critical Thinking, Better Decision Making and Problem Solving*, 2017